KEITH BARRET came to prominence when he recorded a video diary of his work as a mini cab driver, and later a chauffeur, for the BBC series *Marion & Geoff*. He returned to television in 2004 to give relationship advice to a number of celebrity couples on *The Keith Barret Show*. He lives in London but travels extensively around the UK giving motivational talks. He has two children, Rhys and Alun. They live in Cardiff. He would love to hear from them.

Praise for Keith Bar

'A national treasure'

'Hysterically funny … I was almost incapable with laughter'   *Radio Times*

'Achingly funny'   *The Times*

'Sheer comedy brilliance'   *TV Times*

'A stroke of genius'   *Mail on Sunday*

making
divorce
work
IN 9 EASY STEPS

KEITH BARRET

HARPER PERENNIAL
London, New York, Toronto and Sydney

Harper Perennial
An imprint of HarperCollins*Publishers*
77–85 Fulham Palace Road,
Hammersmith
London W6 8JB

www.harperperennial.co.uk

This edition published by Harper Perennial 2005
1

First published by Fourth Estate 2004

'In the Air Tonight' lyrics by Phil Collins;
'People are People' lyrics by Martin Gore of Depeche Mode;
'Celebrate' lyrics by Kool and the Gang.
All reproduced by permission of EMI Music Publishing Ltd,
London WC2H 0EA

Images: 41 Alamy/Private Collection; 44 Alamy;
45 & 46 Getty Stone Images; 144 Paul Duddridge; 148 Alamy

All cartoons by Phil Garner

Graphic on 35 by permission Office for National Statistics

A catalogue record for this book is
available from the British Library

ISBN 0 00 719387 4

Printed and bound in Great Britain by Clays Ltd, St Ives plc

THIS BOOK IS DEDICATED TO GEOFF, MARION
AND MY LITTLE SMASHERS, RHYS AND ALUN,
LIVING THE DREAM.

Contents

Preface

by Paul McKenna

I can honestly say that no other self help author in the world is offering the same advice as Keith Barret.

Foreword

DO YOU WANT THE GOOD NEWS OR THE BAD NEWS?

THE BAD NEWS IS YOU'RE SPLITTING UP...

THE GOOD NEWS IS YOU'RE SPLITTING UP!

NO, I HAVEN'T MADE A MISTAKE;
THAT'S EXACTLY WHAT I MEANT TO SAY.

INTRIGUED?

YOU WILL BE...

I KNOW I AM.

Allow me to introduce myself. My name is Keith Barret. I am a divorced man. **I can honestly say I've never been happier.**

You may not realize it yet but if you are reading this book you are embarking upon one of life's great adventures. In a sense I envy you.

I've called this book *Making Divorce Work,* but you needn't feel left out if you never actually married and all you've done is simply split up with the love of your life, common law spouse, live-in lover, partner, significant other or soul mate. Don't worry. This book is about **failure in all its many forms** and I'm sure it applies just as easily to you.

"So what?" if you're happily married, "So what?" if you're not divorced… What is the opening salvo of any divorce? That's right, the wedding! So even if you're in the happiest place you've ever been and you think your marriage is rock solid, don't worry, any way you look at it you're on the first step towards divorce.

There we are,

DIVORCE

…That word again. It makes some people wince. Why? *Divorce.* Divorce, divorce, divorce… You say it's an ending, I say it's a fresh start. Is the glass half full or half empty? If you're a man who's recently divorced, the chances are you

don't have any glasses left, certainly not the crystal stuff, so come on and join me in raising a beaker to the future!

But before you do, let's first take a **very important step** together as we begin our journey. May I ask you a question? *When was the last time you had an eye test?* That's right, an eye test! A year ago? A week ago? This morning? It really doesn't matter. Regardless of your answer I'm going to put on my optician's hat (they don't have hats do they…? They have those straps with a big-hinged silver disc at the end. Fine, I'll put that on) and prescribe you a new pair of spectacles. But these are **no ordinary glasses** that you can pick up for next to nothing at SpecSavers, nor are they a fancy designer pair of Jeff Banks's from Vision Express, no, they're *magic* glasses and the good news is they're free. Free on the NKS, the National Keith Service!

It's a bit of fun.

That's right, they're not actual glasses at all, they're just **a way of looking at the world**, at life as it goes on around us, a device for getting across my philosophy. I did consider using the more modern and "on message" metaphor of contact lenses but **decided against it** as of course with contact lenses you have to take them out at the end of the day and **soak them** in the bathroom for no less than four hours. I know that you have to take off your glasses also, but the difference is that you can leave them close at hand on the bedside table as you sleep, safe in the knowledge that they're nearby should you need to look at anything in the dark.

So, glasses it is then! But what sort of glasses do I mean? Not rose-tinted ones, that's for sure! I'm a realist, living in the real world, so my glasses need to be real too, so no rose tinting. No, what they are is rose **scented**, so while you see clearly, you're getting the real genuine picture, you're also smelling a lovely scent of roses! Just like an up-market toilet freshener hanging under your nose. I'll be handing you these glasses throughout the book when I want you to see something in a different way. Let's put them on now…

Let's take the word "divorce". In her popular song "D.I.V.O.R.C.E.", country star Tammy Wynette broke the word down into its constituent parts, or letters, coming up with a series of words beginning with each letter. I forget the actual words she came up with and for that I apologize; I had the song on a CD, *The Golden Rhinestone Ladies of Contemporary and Classic Country*, but so far have failed to lay my hands on it… Rest assured though that they, the words, were all rather downbeat and sad. The song was **a massive hit all around the globe**, earning Tammy millions to spend on saddles, but think how much bigger it could have been if she had put, as Tony Blair might say, "a positive spin" on it. If only she'd popped into my opticians for a check-up I could have kitted her out with some special, leather-trimmed Country and Western style glasses! **Tammy missed a great opportunity to show the world the positive, uplifting, life-affirming side of divorce**; but don't worry, I've done it for her…

It's over to Sir Jimmy Saville and Pete Tong in the *Top of the Pops* studio!

"Now then, now then, how's about that then guys and gals, oh, oh, oh! Setting a new record with twenty-five weeks at number one, it's Keith Barret and D.I.V.O.R.C.E.!"

"GREAT!" (PETE).

D: **Dining Out**. Table for one? "Certainly, sir." Watch the bill at the end of the meal shrink before your eyes! Delia had the right idea when she said, "One is Fun!" I'd go a step further: "One is a Lot of Fun!"

I: **Ikea**. Stroll around this Swiss furniture wonderland at your own pace. 10.30 on a Monday morning, the place is very quiet. Stay a few hours and finish off with a slap-up lunch of meatballs and a Dime bar!

V: **Volume**. Turn it up!

O: **Old Friends**. Get on to Friends Reunited and track down your childhood sweetheart. See Step 6, "Respecting a Restraining Order" (Not really, it's a bit of fun…)

R: Restaurants. See D: Dining Out.

C: Christmas. You can do what *you* want to do. So long as it doesn't include the children.

E: Easter. See *Christmas*.

Good? Of course it is. Now then, take off my glasses, read that last bit again and I'm sure you'll think that it's a load of mumbo-jumbo nonsense, so hang on to those imaginary glasses, tie a bit of imaginary string to them and drape them round your imaginary neck like a theatre director or a librarian; you'll be needing them again soon.

Is this book for me?

I think so, yes. Put it this way; **yes it is**. It's for anyone and everyone recently out of a relationship, or anyone and everyone who feels their union may be coming to an end. This book is aimed at anyone and everyone, male or female, hetero or homo, straight or gay.

It's probably most useful to straight men.

That's not important though, what is important is:

**1. That you read on regardless of
your sexual orientation.**

2. Remember that you are not alone.

(What I mean by that is, you *are* alone, you're very alone; but you're not the only one going through it.)

What does it take to make a divorce work?

Well my friend, you may as well ask,
"How long is a piece of string?"

Exactly!

In this case it's nine steps long. How long is a step? In this case **it's about twenty-five pages**, so in this case a piece of string is approximately 224 pages long, including the foreword.

I've broken the whole process of making a divorce work down into nine easy steps, or one long piece of string. I can promise you that by the end of the final chapter you will feel much less like you are staring into an **endless black abyss** contemplating the futility of your own existence. Feelings of humiliation and pointlessness will have been replaced with gaiety and joy. Indeed the only sound of laughter you hear will now be yours, not that of everyone who knows you. If I've done my job, far from avoiding break-up and separation, you'll probably enjoy it! You might even be tempted to enter into a string of doomed relationships just so you can relish the final wrench apart! **This might seem light years away from the uncontrollable sobbing and shaking you're experiencing at**

the moment, but trust me: anything is possible when you've taken the medicine[1] prescribed by Dr Keith![2]

1 Always read the label. (Only joking! It's a bit of fun…)

2 Fourth Estate Legal Notice: At the time of going to press Keith Barret is not a doctor or optician. Fourth Estate in no way endorses any medical or optometric advice dispensed within the pages of this book. All liability rests solely with the author. Consult a qualified medical practitioner before following any of the advice given in this publication.

Introduction

"Hello…"

LIONEL RITCHIE – HELLO

"Hello again"

NEIL DIAMOND – HELLO AGAIN

"Hello, hello, hello, hello, hello, hello…"

THE OASIS – SHAKER MAKER

Good morning, Good morning! What a treat it is to be given the chance to write a book, what's more, a book that people will read, read in their hundreds, in their thousands! Of their own free will, of course, not as part of some huge organized reading. I'm not suggesting that for a moment; I don't see how it could happen, in all honesty, without a degree of force on the part of the organizers, and that's not what I want. Force shouldn't come into it. Yes, the BBC encouraged the nation to pick up books with its excellent serial, *The Big Reader*, but that's all they did, *encourage*. **I don't want a literary apartheid.** When you see what's happening in South Africa, it turns your stomach.

I want people to read this book of their **own free will**, at home, on the bus or maybe in a meadow. Not sitting at rows and rows of desks, undernourished and gaunt with huge jailers looming over them. It would be like a scene from 1984 with John Hurt, a smashing video yes, but hardly the right sort of conditions for enjoying a good read. **And that's what this book should be, above all else, *a good read*, as simple as that.**

Yes, it deals with some very thorny issues, which other authors (I know, unbelievable!) might shy away from, they might think, "Wait a minute, Keith! People might not be able to stomach this. Maybe you should just tell them half the truth…" Well, I'm sorry, but Rome wasn't built like that, **neither was Cardiff**. They don't have *half* buildings, tiny stunted single-storey efforts that only paint *half* the picture; although yes **there are bungalows**, usually retirement properties for the elderly, the infirm or the disabled. In the case of the disabled of course it goes a step further: not only is everything on one floor, all the light switches are lower too, within arm's reach or in some cases they don't have switches, just lots of cords. Cords hanging everywhere. It can look like a thousand party poppers have been set off as part of **a huge celebration** and of course the disabled themselves won't be slow in picking up on the irony of that. We're not here to talk about the disabled, to single them out for special treatment, that's not what they want, they want to be one of the crowd, getting by like everyone else. Unless there are steps in which case nowadays they do expect a ramp. And why not?

It's a bit of fun.

But enough of the fun; let's get back to you and **your problems** and let me say from the outset how thrilled I am to be given the opportunity to enter the world of literature! In all honesty it's the last thing I thought I would do; but why not? Let's have a go…

It was the best of times, it was the worst of times…

Oops! Already taken! Never mind, I'll just think of something new, that's all right; I'm not a writer and would never claim to be. I am, though, a vicious reader. I've just re-read that and realized that I've used the word *vicious* instead of the slightly longer one *voracious*! What a fool. Imagine that, a *vicious reader*! Ridiculous…

Actually, there was a boy at my school, Martin Thorpe, who once pierced the skin on the chest of Mr Deere the English teacher. It happened on a particularly hot day one summer term. Old "no eye" had insisted on keeping the windows shut as he suffered from **an abnormally low body temperature**. As did Mr Pye, the physics teacher; he eventually retired to Chile. I know! Anyway, "no eye" went up to Martin to check on his progress as we read *King Lear* by William Shakespeare. He tapped Martin on his shoulder, whereupon the boy lashed out like a frightened animal, shrieking loudly as he did. Mr Deere recoiled in horror and fell to the ground with Martin's pen sticking out of his chest. I went and helped Mr Deere to his feet and gave Martin back his pen but the damage was done. Martin was suspended for two weeks and Mr Deere retired with nerves.

A Voracious Reader

I've always had a keen interest in reading and as a child was a fully paid up member of the Ladybird Club and **would**

tingle with excitement at the thought of another of their little books plopping through the letter box. I would race out of my room and along the hall, headlong towards the pile of fresh post nestled at the foot of the front door, only to be knocked aside by **my father** as he headed for the same destination. Even though this was long before the days of anthrax in the post, Dad always had a keen sense of protecting his family and was merely checking that the coast was clear before allowing his pride and joy to get too close. He was also keen to check whether that month's *Amateur Rifleman* had come. We would both scurry off with our quarry; Dad to pore over pictures of telescopic lenses and me in my pyjamas to read about Little Red Hen and Chicken Lickin'. Ironically two of the creatures most at risk from Dad's recreational activities.

Great days!

So, anyway, that's enough about me, let's get back to the book and **your feelings of despondency**. It's meant to be what they call a *self-help* book; that is, a book that helps *you* to help *yourself*. I rather think of it though as me helping you, by sharing **my experiences** with you. Experiences garnered from a rich, varied and very happy life that has led me down the road to where I am today. Where am I today? Well, as The Fatboy Slim would say, I'm "*Right Here, Right Now*"! So are you, so what better opportunity for the two of us to get down to work and help each other? **Having said that, it will primarily be *me* helping *you*, as the help is help that comes from me,**

from my experiences. If you tried to help me with the same advice I would have to say that I already know that advice, so "thanks but no thanks", and that probably wouldn't go down well. Let's face it, **if you're reading a self-help book you're not in the best state of mind for handling rejection. Maybe it's a rejection that unpicked the stitching in the fabric of your life and put you in a tailspin in the first place, and my new rejection would just reopen old wounds and encourage you to ponder on the mess you've made of things**. So let's not do that, let's reject it! Let's

REJECT THE REJECTION!

Harsh? Yes, but fair also. I've given it a lot of thought and if I were to accept my own advice from a reader like you, we would just go round in circles, it would be like **teaching an old dog new tricks**. Actually it would be more accurate to say,"teaching a dog in his late 30s (human years, so whatever the equivalent is in dog... times it by seven... 210. Let's face it, at that age you'd be lucky to get a **coherent bark** from him, let alone master a new skill...) tricks of a variety of ages that he already knows", and what would be the point of that? Well all right, yes, I suppose it would enable the old dog to hone the trick, to become even better at it, but...

OK, we could go round the houses forever on this one. For the sake of progress, and so we can be sure that we're shooting from the same hymn sheet, let's say that *I'll* help *you*, end of the story. **You'll be the student and I'll be the master**, like in *Star Wars*, a Jedi and his young Padawan; who knows, maybe one day the tables will turn and the student will become the master, like Darth Vader and Alec Guinness. If so then let's hope that we can remain cordial and content ourselves with a frank exchange of views, with no urge on your part to sever my torso in an act of bitter vengeance...

It's a bit of fun!

"As a child, a good friend of mine had his birthday on the 4th of May. Each year I would write in his card May the Fourth be with you, a bit of fun, and he loved it. This kind of thing is a great way of keeping things light in a friendship. Can you think of any other Star Wars related date gags? Have a go! It's hard, isn't it? I couldn't come up with any."

Off We Jolly Well!

So come on, it's time to start our journey. Seatbelts on, check the mirror, put her in gear, or rather, leave that to me! **You just get yourself comfortable**. Have a look in the glove box, I've left some sweets in there, they're the classic travel sweets in a round tin, lying like broken pieces of Stonehenge in a snowy sherbet field. I like these sweets and always choose them over a more sticky chocolate type affair, in particular because I love the sherbet. I always put a bit of sherbet on my finger and dab it around my nose so that when I glance in the mirror I look like Al Pacino as the cocaine-addled crime lord Michael Corleone in *Scarface*, "Hoo Ha!" A bit of fun, it makes you feel part of the in crowd. **I'm not advocating drug use**, of course I'm not, I must stress that it's not real cocaine, it's the sherbet at the bottom of a **tin of travel sweets**, it's not addictive. If anything I would **urge drug addicts to consider it as an alternative to riding the dragon**; as for those who are toying with the idea of drugs, what I call teetering, I put forward the sweets as a halfway house, a compromise; particularly for teenagers. If you are a teenager I urge you to choose the sweets while at the same time asking what could possibly have gone wrong with your life at such a young age to make you resort to a book like this?

Whatever… This book is open to all comers – academics and idiots, old codgers and young bucks, sober judges and teenage binge drinkers. All are welcome! Let's take the first steps together on our wonderful journey, our fantastic voyage, our magical mystery tour to a place where we will all be…

MAKING DIVORCE WORK!

1

Something's Not Right

But it's OK

"I can feel it coming in the air tonight, oh lord"

PHIL COLLINS – IN THE AIR TONIGHT

"It's not right, but it's OK..."

WHITNEY HOUSTON – IT'S NOT RIGHT, BUT IT'S OK

**"I think I'm done with
the kitchen table, baby"**

GEORGE MICHAEL – OUTSIDE

Picture the scene in your head. Your relationship is ticking over nicely, you are **the happiest man in the world**, you work hard every day and come home every night to a loving cosy home. You think to yourself,

"Keith, it doesn't get better than this."

But in the back of your mind does everything seem *too* perfect? Do you sense something almost imperceptible changing in your loved one, something so other-worldly that it's almost ethereal but none the less it's there? Something so subtle that only you would notice it?

No?

Neither did I.

When it came, it came like a bolt out of the blue. On reflection I wouldn't have had it any other way.

Quick and Painless

Actually in my experience it was quick and pain*ful*. But there you are, pop your glasses on and take a look at that sentence again,

Quick and Painful

Yes it was painful, but it was also quick, *it was over soon*. As George Harrison once said, "*What's that noise? I think there's someone downstairs!*" Not really, only joking, it's a bit of fun… As George Harrison once said, "*All things must pass,*" and this is an important thing to remember when you are in the middle of relationship problems: ***it isn't endless***. It might feel like it is but it isn't. As Bryan Ferry once said, "*Nothing lasts forever, of that I'm sure.*" Having said that *Avalon* is still a cracker.

"The journey of a thousand miles begins with a single step…"

CHAIRMAN MAO – (HE SAID IT)

"To begin at the beginning…"

DYLAN THOMAS – UNDER MILK WOOD

"Begin the Beguine"

JULIO IGLESIAS – BEGIN THE BEGUINE

If you are going to enter into a divorce you have to be like the man at the tollbooth. You have to be **willing to accept change**. That's right, it's a joke, a simple joke and indicative of the sort of humour I'll be peppering throughout the book to alleviate the pain and sorrow and heartbreak.

However, unlike the lowly man in the tollbooth, you won't be looking at small change, you'll be looking at **big change**. Divorce brings with it huge changes, great sweeping changes in all areas of your life, right across the board.

One of the first things to change is the lock.

Like me, you might come home one day and find that your key no longer fits your wife's lock, another man's key now fits. I appreciate how that looks in print but I'm afraid that's not the sort of humour I'm talking about. I'm not denying that it's humorous, of course it is, it's a zinger. The point is that it's *unintentionally* humorous; the double entendre just crept up uninvited and, frankly, unwelcome. If that's the sort of thing you find "amusing" then I'm afraid this book is going to be **a great disappointment** to you.

In all honesty it could be **a great disappointment** on many other levels too, I just don't know. It's my first book and of course I have my doubts as to my ability to "deliver the goods" as they say in publishing, I'd be a fool not to, but that's not going to stop me rolling up my sleeves and jumping in at the deep end. So, no off-colour humour, then. Which is not to say that I'm a prude, because I'm not, not at all. One of the best weekends of my life was a stag weekend in Plymouth for Peter Humphries in 1992. He was marrying a girl he'd met on holiday in Minehead and wanted to have his stag in Plymouth as he'd spent his Easters there as a child. If you've never been, it's a heck of a town, and while there we all went to see Jim Davidson's production of Sinderella. That's right, with an s, *Sin*derella! It was quite **near the knuckle** but I enjoyed it, I really did. Jim was on top form, his usual cheeky self, and I have to say that the sound and lighting were some of the best I've ever seen (and heard) in a theatre,[1] and that

---

1 I should point out that I'm not what you'd call a theatregoer. "What do I mean by that?" I mean that I don't *go to the theatre*. I'm not a culture vulture and I would never claim to be one. Apart from *Sinderella*, one of the last things I saw at the theatre was a wonderful production of *Babes in the Wood*, the pantomime, in Cardiff. I took my two little smashers Rhys and Alyn along and we had a whale of a time. The show starred Lesley Grantham and Vicki Michelle, a top notch cast, and was in the days before Lesley's internet pornography shame when the only shadow on his

includes "We Will Rock You"! It was *that* good. Anyway, the point is, I went and I enjoyed it, so I'm not a prude. However, I don't think that a book like this is the right platform for saucy humour, so if that's what you're looking for I'm afraid it's time to hunt out your receipt. Alternatively, if you haven't yet made your purchase and you're just browsing then please **put down the book and step away from the display**. I'm assuming that you've picked the book up from a stand-alone display, that's what Fourth Estate have promised and I have no reason to doubt them. As for Peter and Jo, it's bad news I'm afraid. They're not together any more, she went to see a hypnotist to give up smoking and… Well, I'm sure you can guess the rest.

---

character was the business with the taxi driver. I always remember the show because I was wearing a ski jacket of all things! I'm not a skier, I would never say I was, but I'd bought this one second hand in a Sue Ryder shop. It was what I call a "puffer" style jacket in a very vivid purple, there was a tear on one arm, just below a sewn-on fabric patch that read, "VALMOREL '95". I was never sure whether it had come from a skier who was disillusioned with skiing after an accident (hence the tear) or whether he was just fashion conscious and deemed it to be a bit "last year". I never got to the bottom of it and to this day am none the wiser. Anyway, the point is I forgot to take the jacket off before the show started and was very hot indeed as basically I was dressed for Alpine conditions. We were sitting in "the Gods", the highest part of the theatre, and I was sweating cobs; I wish you could have seen it, it was unbelievable. At one point Vicki Michelle came out and started to throw chocolates to the kids, a lovely gesture though not quite as generous as it first seems when you consider that the show was sponsored by Cadburys. Rhys and Alyn were egging me on to try and catch some confectionery so I stood up to get a better chance when I was hit in the eye by an Animal Bar. It was quite painful and gave me what doctors call *temporary blindness*. Nonetheless I did manage to drive home with no damage to flesh or bone, though we did lose a nearside wing mirror.

That's right, they broke up, very sad, and it's happening more and more. The figures make for depressing reading; let's dwell on them for a while.

In 2003 there were **143,818** divorces, that's right, one hundred and forty-three thousand, eight hundred and eighteen! Terrible! That's up 1.79% on the previous year. Awful. But it's not all bad news. In the same year there were **249,227** marriages; so *more* marriages than divorces, hurrah! Ah, but wait… that was 7% *down* on the previous year. So… The figures are all over the place, like a see-saw, up and down, round and round… Actually not round and round, they've banned those see-saws, the ones that go round and round, too many accidents in playgrounds, the dark days of concrete flooring, before the springy rubber surface under the swings. And now a lot of them have wood chippings, which are a Godsend, although there again they can disguise the dog dirt and that can lead to all sorts of gastric complications and in some cases, blindness. It's a minefield.

Divorce figures: like a see-saw

One thing is clear, though: any way you slice it, couples are not staying together. Why? Well, there can be many reasons for the break-up of a marriage: infidelity, unfaithfulness, betrayal, these can all play a part.

Death

One reason is the death of a partner. If this has happened to you, **I urge you not to look on it as a *failed marriage***. Don't get me wrong, there has been failure. Statistically speaking, the heart or liver are likely culprits. The figures make for depressing reading; let's have a look at them.

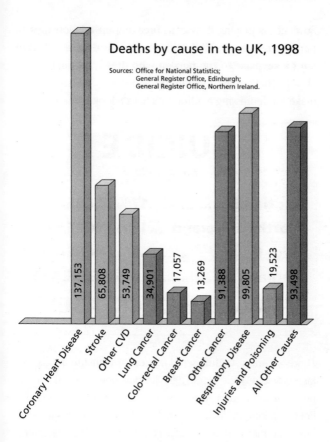

Deaths by cause in the UK, 1998

Sources: Office for National Statistics;
General Register Office, Edinburgh;
General Register Office, Northern Ireland.

Cause	Deaths
Coronary Heart Disease	137,153
Stroke	65,808
Other CVD	53,749
Lung Cancer	34,901
Colo-rectal Cancer	17,057
Breast Cancer	13,269
Other Cancer	91,388
Respiratory Disease	99,805
Injuries and Poisoning	19,523
All Other Causes	93,498

All the usual suspects are there, the big diseases, of course, and poisoning making a return to the spotlight. Stroke is there; I always have a problem with stroke, as it's such a nice word. It's like saying, "How's Tim?" "Oh, haven't you heard? It's awful, he's had a cuddle."

So death is playing its part in breaking up relationships, in particular a certain kind of death, **the kind of death that isn't a surprise to the person who dies**. What am I talking about? That's right. I'm talking about suicide. The figures make for depressing reading; let's have a look at them.

SUICIDE
Since 1990

Scotland ....17% INCREASE

Northern Ireland ....10% INCREASE

Rep. Ireland ....8% INCREASE

England ....6% DECREASE

Wales 7% DECREASE!

There we are, a startling set of figures showing the trends and fashions in suicide since 1990. It's bad news for our friends north of the border in Scotland, where they're leading the field in taking their own lives. Why? It's difficult to say. I suppose that there are many factors to be taken into consideration; the cold weather, poor public transport, etc. At the end of the day **the cause isn't as important as the effect**, and the effect here is quite startling. The Scots are topping themselves with gusto.

"There's a noose loose aboot this hoose!"

It's a bit of fun; we wish them well! Next on the list, our friends in Northern Ireland. This is no surprise really, when you think of the accent. I don't mean to be rude but that awful droning sound, going on and on, it's just terrible; we only hear it when they talk to us but for them it's like that **all the time, even when they're just thinking!** Appalling. No wonder they're reaching for the paracetemol…

Then the Irish themselves, not as bad as their neighbours, and again I put this down to the accent, a far more melodic sound than the northerners, quite cheery and reminiscent of happy days with Leprechauns and the like. You could almost imagine an unemployed Irish man at the end of his tether thinking, "Shall I top myself? Ah begorrah, no! Oil have a pint of Guinness!! Top of the morning to me!"

And The Winner Is…

From top of the morning to top of the pile and the least likely people in Britain to kill themselves are, drum roll please… **the Welsh!** I know! Unbelievable! Well done us! I'm sure that there are many reasons for this but no matter how hard I wrack my brain **I can't think of one**. I expected us to be near the top (or the bottom, depending on how you look at it), what with our reputation for gloominess and all the rain that we have to put up with, but no, if anything we're like a Principality of rugby-playing Gene Kellys, singing in the rain and **smiling through the clouds**.

Actually, this business of the Welsh not wanting to kill themselves is a wonderful example of prejudice and overcoming
it. I'm sure you would have put money on us Welsh being the
most likely to **"do something silly"**, simply because of prejudice. A prejudice that could have been based on nothing
more than a tiny inconsequential incident that occurred
many many years ago. Maybe you once sat next to a very
loud Welsh person on a long arduous train journey, perhaps
you had a very wet weekend camping just outside Tenby or
maybe you're a pop fan and still furious at Welsh music sensation Shakin' Stevens for knocking Bryan Ferry's "Jealous
Guy" off the number one spot in 1981 with "This Ole House".
Maybe you're an *Eats, Shoots & Leaves* kind of person and
your beef with Shaky is nothing to do with his musicianship
and solely based on his maverick spelling of "old". **Whatever the reason, you're prejudiced and that prejudice
is stopping you from seeing the full, clear picture.**

Another thing… My father had a wonderful phrase that he
liked to use: "*Never judge a book by its cover*." It's a zinger,
isn't it? Basically it's saying that appearances can be decep-
tive, things aren't always what they seem, and it's a lovely little
motto to turn to although if I was being picky I would have to
say that the cover *is* probably the best way to judge a book.
Generally speaking the cover tends to hit the nail on the
head with regards to indicating the overall thrust of the book
itself. *Coastal Walks in Pembrokeshire*, for example, is almost
definitely a guide to the many lovely walks that are available
along the Pembrokeshire coast in South Wales, a super

stretch of land with an abundant display of wildlife, particularly birds; and not, I would wager, the story of **one man's struggle against apartheid in South Africa**. That sort of book would probably be called *My Struggle*, *Oppression* or, and this is a good one, *Grey*, meaning the colour you get if you melt black and white together which I would imagine would be the general message of this sort of book. Unless the author was a hard-line militant, hell bent on revenge, in which case it might be *Bloody Hands*, *Boiling Point* or *Die Whitey, Die!*, altogether more hard-hitting titles, again giving a fairly good indication of what's inside and **proof positive that you *can* judge a book by its cover.**

But not always. Here are two tables I've compiled to show you that you have to always be on your guard when it comes to books and covers.

Books That You *Can* Judge By Their Cover

- *The Eyewitness Travel Guide to California*
- *The Radio Times Guide to Films 2004*
- *Dylan Thomas, the Complete Poems*
- *Bruce: The Autobiography of Bruce Forsyth*
- *Green & Black's Chocolate Recipes*

A small selection of books whose titles all give full honest accounts of the material contained within them. Please note that this is just a random selection and *not* a recommendation. However, I have to say that if you *were* looking for a good, solid, reliable, coffee-table-sized reference book on modern cinema and film, you'd have to go a long way to better *The Radio Times Guide to Films 2004*. Now, just to show the other side of the coin…

Books That You *Can't* Judge By Their Cover

- Julia Phillips, *You'll Never Eat Lunch in This Town Again*; NOT an indispensable guide to bad restaurants and cafés, but in fact a fascinating tale of power and excess in Hollywood during the 1970s.
- Martin Amis, *Yellow Dog*; I haven't read it but I'm pretty sure it has nothing to do with Labradors.
- *The Grapes of Wrath*; actually about poor people.
- *A Clockwork Orange*; a very nasty book.

Look Twice…

So Dad was right and wrong at the same time. Let's be clear about something, though: *I'm not saying that my Dad was wrong*, **I would never say that**. I think what his clever little phrase meant was basically "look twice", "don't be so sure". Here's an example of the sort of thing Dad was talking about. We've established that the Scots are far more likely to kill themselves than the Welsh, but look at these two photos:

One was taken in Scotland, the other in Wales; can you guess which is which? Go on, have a go! OK, I'm willing to bet that you think that the one on the bottom is Wales and the one on the top is Scotland, yes? Our survey says... Uh, uh!!! Wrong! It's the other way around, the one on the *top* is Wales and the one on the *bottom* is Scotland! Thanks, Dad, you were right! *Sometimes* you can't judge a book by its cover.

"They seemed so happy..."

Let me ask you another question if I may. How often have you heard a friend or relative say, "Guess who's splitting up?" and then when he or she tells you who it is, it comes as a complete shock? That's right, lots of times, we all have. Why is it such a shock?

Because it's a surprise. (Figure 9)

Fig. 9

These days, with divorce rates soaring, it is almost impossible to predict which couples will stay together and which ones will split up.

Or is it? Try this little quiz to see how good you are at spotting who will stay together "'til death do us part".

If I were to tell you that I had devised a method that could predict the success of a marriage, based purely on a detailed analysis of photographs taken on the wedding day, would you be interested? I thought so! Then read on…

On the following three pages are photographs of three couples on their wedding days. All seemingly happy pictures of young, healthy men and women on the most important day of their lives, with their futures together ahead of them, the hopes and dreams of their respective families held in their conjoined arms; but which if any will end in tears? I want you to study the pictures closely and see if you can spot any clues to help you predict which of the couples are still together. **Maybe by doing so you will be able to choose more wisely yourself next time!** It's a bit of fun.

N.B. All the weddings took place in 1995. I'm writing this in 2004, so **they've all passed the dreaded seven-year itch!**

Right, couple number one. Look closely at them and see what you can see in their faces. Future happiness? Despair? **A bit of both?** Quite a posh wedding in that they have doves although I must say that from only looking at the picture it's difficult to be sure whether they're releasing the doves or desperately trying to catch them.

These seem like a very happy couple, or did they also have doves, and store them too close to an extractor fan? Are the newlyweds about to look to the sky and come face to face with feathered carnage? We'll never know and it doesn't matter. Let's just savour the moment of happiness captured forever.

Hmm, yes, I know what you're thinking… Less a case of, "Are they still together?" and more, "Is she still alive?"

Now that you've seen all the photos of the happy couples, let me give you a word of advice: **Look at them again**. Are there any telltale signs that you've missed? Body language enthusiasts can have a field day with this kind of thing. Look at the way the couples stand: is there an uneasy air to any of them? The way they're standing, peculiar looks on faces, what does this tell us? Can you spot a distance or awkwardness, an underlying tension? **Have any of the men got beards?** My Uncle Gethyn had a beard and he did eighteen months for misappropriation of council funds.[2]

Study very closely; **think of yourself as a detective**, Inspector Morse with Lewis, Hercule Poirot with his wax moustache or maybe Miss Marple with her cardigan combing a crime scene for vital clues. Not that the pictures contain any crimes, I'm not claiming that for a minute, of course I'm not. Having said that, in all honesty at the end of the day we don't

2 Gethyn, an avid Beatles fan, worked for Cardiff City Council and organized a trip to Hamburg, birthplace of The Beatles (but surprisingly, not the hamburger!) on council business. He was thrilled that he would finally walk in the footsteps of his heroes, having already visited Liverpool and had his photograph taken by the "Penny Lane" road sign and walked past the Dakota Building in New York during a Fly Drive in America. The trip itself was a great success and Gethyn received all the plaudits; we'd never seen him happier. **Three months later he was charged and found guilty of misappropriation of council funds and sentenced to eighteen months in prison**, although he only served nine of those on account of his **good behaviour**. (He is credited with implementing the Dewey Decimal System in the Prison Library and introducing the Governor to Gilbert and Sullivan.) On his release his marriage crumbled and he lost his job. Five years later he has remarried, lives in Guildford, and drives an Audi. It never rains…

know. **We could easily be looking at no more than a parade of particularly cunning bigamists**, or three at the most. I think it unlikely that there would be more than three in our selection, as it would mean that some of them had married each other, bigamist on bigamist, and that surely is **a statistical rarity**. In its defence though I would say that it probably eases the pain of discovering that your husband/wife is a bigamist if you already are one yourself; it would give you a certain empathy. "Fair enough, I know how he/she feels…". Still, any way you slice it you would have been deceived, lied to, conned, and no one likes that, it can leave you with **a distrust of your fellow human beings that can stay with you for the rest of your waking days.**

Back to the quiz! Which couples are still together and which ones have parted? Have you made up your mind? OK, turn to page 52 to find out, I think it will shock you…

Role-play

Welcome to our first role-play. Role-playing is a vital part of understanding relationships and can be a great tool to unlock the door to the mystery of happiness. The role-plays that I have created are all for two players, usually a man and a woman although at the time of writing I am in talks with my publishers about a gay role-play. More news on that when I have it, but don't hold your breath…

The role-plays will occur at the end of each step and will serve as an opportunity to recap on what we've (you've) just learnt, allowing us (you) to almost experience the **emotions, feelings and frustrations** expressed in the chapter, viewing them from your own unique perspective. One slight word of warning though: role-plays are traditionally best when acted out by more than one person. The very fact that you are reading this book suggests there is every chance that you are on your own. If this is the case, don't despair (any more than you already do about everything else in your life). If you have been separated for any length of time you will now be the proud owner of the greatest gift that solitude can bring, that is **A VIVID IMAGINATION.** Now is your opportunity to reap the harvest of endless days picturing dates, times, scenarios and, most importantly, third parties. So, curtain up, lights, cameras… ACTION!

The Roles: **Brad***, 39, tall, tanned, good-looking tennis pro. You are a happy, easy-going man, proud father of two small boys, the apples of your eye. You spend much of your time, when not on the court, looking after your little smashers and getting the house ready for your wife,* **Jennifer***.*

Jennifer*, you are 38, an attractive busty woman who can be misunderstood as being somewhat sharp tempered but are, in fact, deep down a warm, caring, lovely individual.*

The Scenario: Home.

Jennifer *has been coming home later and later every night for the last month, she smells of cigarettes and alcohol and is* *secretive about the text messages she receives in the early hours of the morning. You are woken by the sound of her falling into the bedroom at 3 a.m.*

This role-play shows the moment when both players realize that something isn't right.

*N.B. The role-playing is multiple choice! You may be trying this exercise on your own; if that is the case it's a good idea to denote the different characters within the role-play clearly and concisely. One way is this: for **Brad** sit down, for **Jennifer**, stand up, puff out your chest and loom over **Brad.***

BRAD Hello, love, where have you been? I have suspicions regarding your recent behaviour.

JENNIFER What?

BRAD I said, "Where have you been? I have suspicions regarding your recent behaviour."

JENNNIFER Are you talking to me?

BRAD Yes.

JENNIFER What?

BRAD What?

JENNIFER What did you say?

BRAD I said, "What?"

JENNIFER No, before that…

BRAD I said, "Yes."

JENNIFER No, before that…

BRAD I said I have suspicions about your recent behaviour.

JENNIFER Brad, for heaven's sake, you have to believe me. I love you and I always will…

OK, so far so good, but this is the crucial stage, the turning point in the role-play, the moment at which the relationship could go either way. So how do you respond to Jennifer? What is your reaction? Do you believe her and pledge to start again, putting the past and all the distrust behind you once and for all? Or do you stand firm in your belief that she's a bit of a hussy and not to be trusted? I've set out three possible responses, each taking a different emotional and psychological standpoint; which would you choose? Would you say…

• A: What the hell are you talking about? I can't believe you, I won't believe you and I don't believe you! You're a busty charlatan, a floozy and a tramp! My mother was right, I should never have married you! Get out of the bedroom, get out of the house, get out of my life!

• B: We need to talk over our problems in an adult, responsible manner. I've made an appointment with a relationship therapist for us both on Thursday night.

• C: Have we got any milk?

Which did you choose? What do you think your choice says about you? I would like to be able to help you at this stage but of course it's **impossible for me to know** which of the three options you chose. That's a shame because I think this would be a wonderful opportunity for learning together. I did talk to my publishers about trying to develop an interactive element to the book, a *Big Brother* phone vote, a *Who Wants to be a Millionaire* "Press your buttons now!" moment or at the very least the big red and green pepper cards from *Ready, Steady, Cook*. Alas it wasn't to be. We did work together for a while on some mini pepper cards but it was felt that they might lend the book a "novelty" feel that could work against us in the long run. We could end up looking like the sort of book you'd find in your stocking at Christmas and not, as I hope, a book that you'd find in the Academic section of the bookshop and one that will in the fullness of time be added to the National Curriculum.

NOW I KNOW

* The Welsh are happier than the Scots.

* You can sometimes judge a book by its cover.

* Uncle Gethyn found happiness in Guildford.

ANSWER TO WEDDING DAY QUIZ: I don't know! I've got absolutely no idea, none whatsoever. I got the pictures off the Internet. It's a mystery, an absolute mystery, but **that's my point!** The Mystery of Marriage… there is NO WAY ON EARTH of predicting who will stay together and who will split up.

It's a
Family Affair

And We're All Family Now

"We are family"
SISTER SLEDGE – WE ARE FAMILY

"Don't cry Daddy"
ELVIS PRESLEY – DON'T CRY DADDY

"He's the greatest dancer"
SISTER SLEDGE – HE'S THE GREATEST DANCER

Divorce has never been so popular! The statistics prove a remarkable fact – that children of divorced parents are more likely to then go on to experience divorce themselves.

In that sense divorce can be like an heirloom – a vase, a painting or in my case a rifle, handed down from generation to generation.

Proud Mary

Approaching the subject from this viewpoint we can see divorce as **something to be very proud of**, particularly for the already divorced parent of the divorcing child as they see their offspring carrying on the family tradition. In a society that moves faster and faster and seems so impersonal, parents are searching for **something to pass on to their children**. In the past, **one of the most significant things would have been their trade** and this would have been reflected in their name.

For example we would know that Tommy *Cooper's* ancestors

were barrel makers, and this skill would have been passed down from father to son. In the television series *Porridge*, Norman Stanley *Fletcher's* ancestors would have made arrows, and the man who played him, Ronnie *Barker*, would have come from a long line of dog handlers. **We *Barrets* have prided ourselves in the manufacture of low-cost, high-quality starter homes**. Not really.

It's a bit of fun!

The point is that the name was a source of pride to the family because it told the world so much about them. Nowadays it is the same but different. We can still learn a lot about a person from their name, e.g. we know when a person has four or five children with different surnames then it's highly likely **that family has experienced divorce**, or at the very least, separation. This is not the whole of the story, though. A person can choose to buck the trend and change the course of the family tradition; it is with no small amount of pride that I, Keith Barret, am the first in my family to sip from the golden goblet of divorce! (Immediate family, I'm not including Gethyn.) Just because your parents are happy, contented and facing their twilight years bathed in the rosy glow of companionship, that's **no reason for you not to embark on the safari of separation that is divorce**.

That Pioneer Spirit

There are some who see my situation (and others like me,

people like you) as a failure. Fine, as Bobby Brown would say, "that's their prerogative",[1] **I prefer to see us as pioneers**, charting a brave new world of happiness and opportunity. Particularly in my case as **I come from parents who *didn't* divorce**, they stayed devoted to each other right to the end. It was much harder for me therefore to make that break with tradition and begin walking down a different path. **How much easier it would have been if I'd come from a broken home, to then go and break one myself.** If this is ringing bells with you, then take heart. Just because divorce was beyond your parents **doesn't** mean that it's beyond you. It won't be easy; you'll have to dig deep inside your heart for inspiration as you take your family tree in a new direction.

---

1 Bobby Brown, "My Prerogative", (1989) *Bobby Brown's Greatest Hits*, MCA Records.

Speaking of family trees, divorcing can be a wonderful way of adding colour and variety to the tree, as it struggles to cope with the new sprouting offshoots that point outwards with new names and faces. **Keen gardeners** will get a kick out of this and a sense of genetic topiary as they prune and trim their own trees, letting their creative instincts run riot amongst the heartbreak and emotional chaos.

Why Not Me?

In an age when so many marriages end in divorce, we find ourselves with the odd situation of **the normal becoming the unusual** and what once was **the unusual now becoming the normal**. What I mean by that is that whereas it was once normal for couples to stay together it is now more likely that they won't and so it is **the families of the couple that stay together that can feel the stigma of being *different***. It is far easier nowadays to divorce and to live your life as a divorced person or as the friend or immediate family of a divorced person.

This can lead to great problems for the friends and families of those couples who have chosen not to divorce and can lead to the syndrome known as *Why Not Me?*, or *The Why Not Me? Syndrome*, or *WNMS*. This is a feeling of **exclusion**, a feeling of **not fitting in**, a sense of **not belonging**, and can prove **quite debilitating**. For our purposes in this step we are concerned primarily with the WNMS experienced when our parents didn't divorce but stayed together. Typically, the child of this sort of marriage will have experienced a set of conditions similar or identical to those detailed below:

- Happy, contented well-matched parents.
- A feeling of security and emotional well-being.
- Rosy glow childhood memories.
- A lack of psychological intricacies or *hang-ups*.
- Joyous family get-togethers/meals/reunions.
- Wise advice.
- Frequent telephone conversations with parents.

These conditions will be more than familiar to sufferers of *Happy Parent, Why Not Me? Syndrome,* or *HPWNMS.*

HPWNMS
(Happy Parent, Why Not Me? Syndrome)

Case Study

For the purposes of this case study I have reprinted a letter I received from Angela Coulthard, a twenty-eight-year-old lady, living in Kent. She has a good job, a loving husband, two daughters that she dotes on and a top-of-the-range Chrysler car with power steering and tinted windows. Yet she feels unhappy. She mentions her parents in her letter and their plans for another trip to Egypt, even after a pair of hip replacement operations! There's also an offer for Angela and her family to go with them on the trip. Here's Angela to tell us more…

Dear Keith,

I am a 28-year-old lady, living in Kent. I have a good job, a loving husband, two beautiful daughters on whom I dote and a Chrysler Grand Voyager with power steering and tinted windows. On the surface I seem to have everything. So why am I so unhappy? It's not as if I come from a broken home. My parents recently celebrated forty happy years together and even after joint hip replacement operations are currently planning their second trip to Egypt; they've even offered to take us along!

Why am I not happy?

Please help...

Yours,

Angela Coulthard

This letter is typical of many that I have received and high-lights an alarming case of Happy Parent, Why Not Me? Syndrome. Angela, if you're reading this (I didn't reply), please don't despair, I'm about to show you that **you're not alone** and that there are steps you can take to escape this **jungle of contentment**. She points out that she doesn't come from "a broken home"; that's OK, it doesn't matter. I myself am not the product of a broken home but that didn't stop me from producing one. It's all part of HPWNMS; here's some background:

Sufferers of HPWNMS find themselves increasingly marginalized in today's society. All around they see images of parental discord: in the newspapers, on the radio, on the soap operas, families split up and torn asunder, tears, anger and recrimination. Vows broken, promises forgotten, irons thrown; at home they see nothing of the sort. It is said that people watch the soaps for many reasons, not least to see themselves reflected on the screen, to see their lives writ large. In the old days this was possible. Think of the idyllic family set-up portrayed in *The Waltons*, *Little House on the Prairie*, even *Upstairs Downstairs* with its now outdated class-ridden hierarchical household, nevertheless showed people basically getting on, up to a point. This gave the unhappy in society something to aspire to and the happy something to identify with. Nowadays the television is a constant source of conflict, from Albert Square to The Rovers Return, even genuinely ground-breaking television programmes like *Changing Rooms* often end in a furious bust-up.

It is easy to see how the happy child of happy parents can begin to experience feelings of alienation and unease, made all the worse by the fact that these feelings are occurring **while the person is happy**. Therefore adding **confusion** to the list of problems. So what can be done for these people? Some would say that they should see their situation for what it is, **something to be proud of**. I say differently. Once again I'm going to step outside the envelope; I'm going to come at it from a different angle. It's time to put on your glasses again:

If You Can't Beat Them, (un) Join Them

Exactly! If you can't beat them, join them! That's right, **a happy marriage is no reason for it to last for ever. The only way you are going to feel like one of the crowd is if your parents divorce!**

But how?

How can you take a happy, contented marriage and plant within it the seeds of despair and heartbreak?

How can you take your parents' rock solid foundations and **smash them into ten thousand tear-stained pieces**? How can you split a happy contented twosome that seemed to be joined at the hip – sometimes, as with Angela's parents, joined at the new plastic hip? How do you take their old-fashioned anti-social togetherness and turn it in to contemporary displaced alienation and discord? It's easy if you know how, and I'm about to tell you! **I won't rest until your parents are parted and fitting in with society. Until their circle of friends has been split down the middle, until family members have been divided and until Dad is living in a bedsit!**

The first thing to realize is that there is no *universal adaptor, one size cure all*. When trying to destroy a happy marriage the technique must be tailored exclusively to the couple in question. **Ignore this advice** at your peril. A friend of mine, Iestyn Jones from Cardiff, once tried to break up his parents' blissfully happy marriage, for the very reasons outlined earlier. He considered himself to be suffering from HPWNMS and set about formulizing a plan of attack. On the surface his plan appears to be a sure-fire winner.

Iestyn's Plan

1. Introduce his father to Mary Collins, local florist and choir member.

2. Engineer moments when the two can be alone.

3. Encourage consumption of alcohol at florists to "loosen up" the pair.

4. Confirm the beginning of an "intimate relationship".

5. Establish a pattern of liaisons, noting time, location, etc…

6. Drive mother to location and allow her to stumble on to the scene.

At first glance this plan appears foolproof. It has a fiendish, almost criminal mastermind quality to it and would not seem out of place in a fast-moving Matt Damon film like *The Bourne Identity*. However, this plan was to prove about **as wrong as wrong can be** and validates my theory that any plan "*must be tailored exclusively to the couple in question*".

Iestyn thought that by introducing a scarlet woman into the equation he would **undermine the foundations of his**

parents' marriage and bring inescapable feelings of jealousy and distrust between his mum and dad. What he didn't realize was that the very thing he thought would destroy his parents' marriage was actually the one ingredient that had been missing. **A more exotic sex life!** On stumbling into the back room of the florists that fateful Tuesday afternoon in May, Glenda (Iestyn's mum) opened up a whole new and exciting chapter in an otherwise fading marriage.

Only recently I received an e-mail from Iestyn telling me that Mary the florist has now moved in with his parents and that the three of them have joined a nationwide internet-based swingers' network, regularly hosting evenings of *fun and games* at their modest semi in Chepstow and organizing trips to the theatre. Most recently Michael Ball singing "Songs from the Shows" at the Bristol Hippodrome. **Iestyn says his parents have never been closer and just last month his dad had a pacemaker fitted so that he can keep up with Mary and Glenda!**

He regrets ever tinkering with his parents' marriage and feels that, if anything, things have got worse. So it just goes to show that what would work a treat for one couple would not work for another. Think on!

In the Club!

Here is a list of names, a simple, mid-length list. Read the list and then see if you can tell me what they have in common.

- Angelina Jolie
- Billy Zane
- Britney Spears
- Brooke Shields
- Carrie Fisher
- Cher
- Courtney Love
- Drew Barrymore
- Elle Macpherson
- Elvis Presley
- Eminem
- George Clooney
- Gillian Anderson
- Halle Berry
- Janet Jackson
- Jeff Goldblum
- Jennifer Lopez
- Jim Carrey
- Johnny Depp
- Julia Roberts
- Kate Winslet
- Lenny Kravitz
- Madonna
- Michael Jackson
- Nicole Kidman
- Pamela Anderson
- Robert Downey Jnr
- Tom Cruise
- Tom Hanks
- Uma Thurman
- Will Smith

Well, any ideas? **Famous?** Yes, that's true, they are famous. **Attractive?** Yes again, they are, almost all of them, attractive. **Actors**, **actresses** or **singers**. Yes that's also true, but what else links them? Because that's not what I'm looking for. The zodiac? Are they all the same star sign? No they're not.[1] The answer? OK…

THEY HAVE ALL BEEN DIVORCED!

1 They might be, I haven't checked it out. I think it's unlikely though.

I know, unbelievable! A list of fantastically successful people, but that's not what links them; **what links them is divorce!** Think about it. They're all part of the same club as you! Are they all parents? I don't know. Some of them certainly are, others I'm not so sure; it doesn't matter. Were their parents divorced? Again, I'm not sure, I got these names from the internet, and researching the marital history of the mothers and fathers was a step too far, I'm afraid. Let's **assume** that some of them had parents who divorced and you can see how potent my HPWNMS theory is!

Angelina Jolie married Jonny Lee Miller in 1993 and then divorced in 1999, a six-year marriage. She then went on to find happiness with Billy Bob Thornton. **Billy Zane**, the nasty, wig-wearing husband of Kate Winslet (see **Kate Winslet**) in *Titanic* got married to Lisa Collins in 1988 and divorced in 1995: iceberg! **Britney Spears** married Jason Allen Alexander in 2004. (Not the Jason Alexander that plays George in *Seinfeld*, a different, presumably younger and hairier one…) They were divorced two days later! What can have gone wrong?

The mind boggles. **Brooke Shields** married Andre Agassi in 1997 then divorced in 1999: new balls! **Carrie Fisher** (Princess Leia in *Star Wars*) married Paul Simon in 1983 and divorced in the same year; since then it's been *the sound of silence* between them.

Too Many Jokes

Actually, I've just realized what I've done: I've inadvertently started detailing all the people on the list and putting a little joke after each one. In all honesty **I don't think I can keep it up**, I think I've painted myself into a corner, humour wise. If it's all the same with you I'll withdraw gracefully. It's a shame because there are a few jokes that come to mind for some of them. I could say something about **Cher** having to *share* the assets after the divorce. With **Jeff Goldblum** I could say, "I'd like to have been a **fly** on the wall at that wedding!" (Jeff was in a film called *The Fly.*) Good gags, but not enough for the whole of the list. That's OK, I'm not a comedian, this is not a comedy book, it's a self-help book. Some of you may have come here looking for laughter after seeing one of my TV appearances when I readily admit I have made jokes in the past. But one swallow does not a summer make! I have a similar problem when people come to see me talk on my nationwide tours; because that is what I do, I talk. It's not a show; it's a talk. A lot of people who come expecting a show go away bitterly disappointed. Having said that, a lot of the people who come expecting a *talk* also go away bitterly disappointed. There we are, you can't please everyone. On one fateful night on the tour, in King's Lynn, I think it was fair to say that I couldn't please *anyone*. A dreadful night that I hope I never see repeated... Dreadful for me, dreadful for the audience and dreadful for the St John's Ambulance people who did an excellent job in very difficult circumstances. You've heard of **stage diving**, when a young pop star will hurl himself headlong off the stage and into the audience? Well, this was almost a complete reversal of that.

NOW I KNOW

* Just because your parents didn't divorce doesn't mean that you can't.

* Jeff Goldblum was in *The Fly*.

* Humour is best handled by professional comedians.

* The people of King's Lynn are quick to turn.

3

What Iceberg? (Death on Denial)

Facing the Facts of Failure

"I don't wanna know"

JOHN MARTYN – I DON'T WANNA KNOW

"I don't want to talk about it"

ROD STEWART – I DON'T WANT TO TALK ABOUT IT

"Don't"

ELVIS PRESLEY – DON'T

In his book *How To Mend Your Broken Heart* (Bantam Press £7.99) Paul McKenna writes, "*The Buddhists say that our hearts are meant to be broken because that is how they open. From that point of view it would be a great sadness to get through life without having your heart broken at least once.*"
I think this is a bit harsh, saying that you can only open something by breaking it. **What about Tupperware?** Please be clear on this, I'm not having a go at Paul McKenna, I'm not having a go at Tupperware, **I'm having a go at the Buddhists**.

I would never have a go at Mr McKenna, I'm a big fan of his and remember sitting glued to my TV with my heart in my mouth as he sat suspended above the Thames in his Perspex box. The problem with Paul McKenna's advice is a very simple one in my view and it is this: **It comes from Paul McKenna!** Do you see? Paul McKenna is a celebrity and as such is not subject to the emotional ups and downs, insecurities and uncertainties that can plague ordinary people like you and me. His is a high-octane life lived at a breakneck pace (witness his brilliant performance in the Star in a Rea-

sonably Priced Car feature on BBC2's *Top Gear!*), it bears
little or no relation to the more humdrum existence enjoyed
by you or I. Whereas you or I, when we wake up in the morning, might think, "Hmm, what'll it be? Cornflakes or Weet-
abix?" Paul is more likely to pad about his **shag-pile** carpet
wondering whether to call Jay Kay from Jamiroqui, Paul
Young or indeed Jeremy Clarkson and invite them round for
breakfast on his roof terrace; it's that kind of life, one of
excess and indulgence.

And yet as I read those words back I'm not so sure!
Maybe he's right, maybe the Buddhists are right, maybe Paul
McKenna **is** a Buddhist! I must stress I don't know if he is, that's
his private business and it should remain so until he decides
to go public, probably in the form of a book entitled *How to
Become a Buddhist in 7 Days!* I must say that if he does put his
remarkable mind to it and takes the plunge it wouldn't surprise me and let's face it he's half way there already with his
trendy close-cropped hairstyle. In all honesty, and I'm sure he
wouldn't mind me saying so, that's more the result of our old
friend MPB, male pattern baldness, than any higher level of
spiritual enlightenment! And anyway, why would Paul want to
look like Buddha? For all that people harp on about it being
the route to eternal wisdom, you'd have to say that Buddha
himself is more than a little overweight! I don't know whether
they have the facilities for cholesterol and fat ratio testing in
the backwaters of Tibet but if they did there'd be a nasty shock
in store for the CEO of the Buddhist Faith. Of course one of the
first things any qualified medical practitioner would recom-

mend would be **a less stressful, more placid lifestyle**. Try telling that to Buddha! His jolly face would redden with rage and then, like a very fat Mike Reid from *EastEnders*, he'd probably say, "You're 'avin a laugh!" And quite right too!

So no, **Paul McKenna is not Buddha**, but he *is* a mystical man and he *does* have undeniable powers of the mind. Try saying otherwise to the literally hundreds of people who enjoy his regular tours of the UK with his Hypnotic Show. On the night I went, he had a capacity crowd at the Becks Theatre in Hayes in the palm of his hand. Bravo! Encore! He's a **very mystical man** and if I had to liken him to any great spiritual leader it would be **the Dalai Lama**; albeit a Gucci-clad, healthier-looking Dalai Lama with a voice that could sell sand to the Arabs. Or at the very least Kenco Coffee to housewives in a mid-morning ad break on a British commercial radio station like Heart or Classic FM.

An Act of Faith

So let's go with Paul and those crazy Buddhists for a moment, let's put our naturally cautious, wary nature to one side and give them their head and explore what they have to say, because when you think about it, it does make sense… *"The Buddhists say that our hearts are meant to be broken because that is how they open. From that point of view it would be a great sadness to get through life without having your heart broken at least once."* Yes! I like it! I really do! **Isn't that what we all want to do, to "open our hearts"?** As long ago as

1986 Madonna was imploring us to do just that[1] with her catchy infectious song of the same name.

Madonna is of course one of the world's most celebrated spiritual people, living in the eye of a hurricane, with pop madness going on all around her in a heady whirl, she none the less manages to find twenty minutes every day for her yoga. It is this yoga, combined with her new religion Kaballah, that has helped her grow as a person and particularly as an artist. From singer to actress and more recently to author, just like Spicy Geri Halliwell, she conquers each new challenge with ease. This is nowhere more evident than in her work as a bestselling author and I'm willing to bet that it's her love of Kaballah that has helped her make the difficult transition from coffee-table photo books of hardcore pornography to children's fiction in such a seamless and graceful manner. But how do you "open your heart"? Do you *have* to break it or can you prise, twist or pop it open? It's no good asking Madonna, she's too busy to answer; allow me to have a crack at it…Well, I suppose it's different for every couple. As the saying goes, "There's more than one way to skin a dead cat!" Certainly, if you and your partner view your relationship as a dead cat then even a layman would say you're on shaky ground to begin with and that your desire to "skin" it will only add to the upset… However, the saying still stands as an analogy in as much as it says that there is more than one way to "open your heart" and let the love in.

1 Madonna,"Open Your Heart", from her brilliant album, *Now That's What I Call Music 8*

Each couple will want to find a way that is right for them. How many times have you heard a happy couple talking about an aspect of their richly fulfilling life and then saying, "It wouldn't be right for everyone, but it's right for us…"? Why is this? Well, it's because people are different. But don't take my word for it; try this little experiment.

Experiment

1. Get up from the chair you're sitting in and take a walk down your street.

2. Look at the houses as you pass them, paying close attention to the doors.

3. Now look beyond the structure of the doors and concentrate instead on their colour or hue. Allow your eye to examine every inch of the door, its frame, its body, its letter box, its knocker.

4. Now take out your note pad and write down the colour of the door (I should have mentioned at the start to take a pad and pencil/pen with you, sorry). Do this until you have ten colours corresponding to ten doors.

5. Now return home.

6. Once home, sit down on a favourite chair and slowly read back the listed colours.

7. I can't be 100% sure but I'll guess that the list reads something like this:

> Black
> Green
> Black
> Red
> Blue
> Black
> Green
> Purple
> Red
> Brown (Natural)

1. On first reading the list seems to have a random, chance-like quality to it, with no detectable predetermined pattern to speak of.

2. Read it again.

3. On your second reading there should still appear to be no predetermined pattern. Why? **Because there isn't one.** It's just a random collection of colours, BUT it proves a very important point.

> *"So we're different colours*
> *And we're different creeds*
> *And different people*
> *Have different needs"*
> DEPECHE MODE – PEOPLE ARE PEOPLE

So sang Davey Gahan and the boys way back in 1984 and they were right, we're different! Each and every one of us. My simple experiment proves it once and for all. **We are all doors**, and we are all painted in different colours, all the colours of the rainbow, though predominantly white, black, brown and yellow; and like doors we are all waiting to be opened. But how, with our odd foibles, traits and quirks, **how can we open ourselves up fully, not just ajar?**

How do we let the love in?

"Celebrate good times come on!"

KOOL AND THE GANG – CELEBRATE

One of the first things to do is to recognize the fact that we're different and to accept it. All right, I'll go further than that, I'll go out on a limb. We should *celebrate* our differences! So you've got a wonky nose, so what? So you stammer when you talk, so what? So you don't like cheese, who cares? **It's these little differences that make us special**. When I was at school, there was a boy in the year above me, Mark Thomas, who had a peculiar way of talking. Because of the way his teeth were aligned, every time he spoke an "s" sound he made a whistling noise. Speech therapists would tell you that this is called a "sibilant s" and indeed it is. They will also tell you that it is quite common and that it can, to a degree, be corrected through speech therapy. Mark took great comfort from this and never let his sibilance get him down; to him it simply wasn't a big deal.

However, to some of the other, bigger boys in his year it *was* a big deal and they **bullied him mercilessly**, making his school life a **living hell**. It got so bad that his family moved out of the area. Mark's father worked for a large company and was lucky enough to be relocated to the historic English spa town of Bath, this was after a short-lived spell in Cirencester which, given his defect, only added insult to injury; I remember him standing up to the bullies at school one spring morning and telling them where he was going to go. They pretended they couldn't hear and forced him to repeat his destination over and over. What ensued was like a scene from *Apocalypse Now*; poor Mark came within inches of losing his life. Once in Bath, a lovely rural setting and perfect for a fresh start, you would have thought that things would get better. Alas it wasn't enough for Mark and he deteriorated rapidly. The sibilance worsened, developing into **a kind of spitting action** and soon Mark became ostracized. I recently went to Bath by train[1] to see the redevelopment of the Roman Baths and actually saw Mark loitering outside the

1 Rather surprisingly, this was a very enjoyable journey. Paddington Station looks magnificent since its refit, it now has an almost Neapolitan feel, the staff were very helpful and there was a welcome lack of youths in hooded tops drinking from cans. Once on the train itself, things went from good to better, it was like being in that advert where the chess piece curls up and goes to sleep! I got talking to a man from Yeovil who had just tracked down his twin brother after thirty-seven years apart, he said they'd been reunited at a Gloucester pub and much to his surprise they hadn't got on at all. We sped on to Bath, stopping only for one delay, a fatality on the track near Stroud. Suicide or murder? The inquest will decide.

entrance with a dog on a string. I noticed with some sadness that his own grubby boots and the paws of his furry companion were both drenched in saliva.

A great shame and a lesson I suppose that sometimes it's *not* a good idea to celebrate your differences, but I like to think that Mark's depressing decline into madness is the exception that proves the rule and therefore I would still urge you to celebrate yours! Or as Mark might say, "Thelebrate yourth!" It's a bit of fun.

Going, Going … Gone!

Some people see the breakdown of their marriage as a failure. They feel stigmatized by divorce, feel that they've scarred their children irrevocably and have disappointed their parents and caused heartbreak all around.

And to a degree they have.

But I don't see it like that. Remember when I mentioned my special glasses, earlier in the book? It's time to whip them out again!

Being married is a lot like being at an auction. Think of your spouse as the "lot" for which you are bidding; what's very popular now of course is what I call the "online" auction, when people auction things on the World Wide Web or internet. The leader in this field is eBay. So if you have lost your spouse, or "lot", to another, don't look on it as a rejection, as a pitiless swipe at your inadequacy, as a reinforcement of your own feelings of worthlessness. Not at all! **Think of it simply as being outbid!** This should take some of the sting out of it for you. Then, later on when you are out on the town, looking for love, why not follow the thought process through and think of yourself as a "lot" too? Then, if you find it hard to meet a new partner you can always comfort yourself with thinking that bidders have simply failed to meet your reserve price! You're out of their league!

There's probably some off-colour humour to be had at this point from references to "banging your gavel" but as I stated very clearly in an earlier section, this is **not that sort of book**. If you are looking for some off-colour humour, then that's fine, I'm not criticizing you or judging you. What I call "being judgemental", not at all; in fact if you turn to the bibliography at the back of the book you'll find a whole extensively researched section devoted to that sort of publication, which I hope will point you in the right direction. "Thank you, Keith." You're welcome!

Death on Denial

That's the sub-heading for this chapter, it's a pun, a play on words, a good way of getting the reader's attention as we move into a difficult area together. Regular crossword puzzlers, word searchers or viewers of *Countdown* will have no trouble in cracking the code and seeing what the pun is referring to, but for the rest of us, rather than lose some of the slower readers at this early stage I think I should perhaps explain.

DEATH ON DENIAL   **DEATH ON THE NILE**

That's right! It's a reference to the Agatha Christie film with Peter Ustinov as Hercule Poirot solving crimes on a boat! But it's not just the late Peter Ustinov who has brought Mr Poirot vividly to life; in the UK we regularly enjoy David Suchet (*Executive Decision, Harry and the Hendersons*, brother reads the news…) in the role. There's also been Martin Gabel (*Lord Love a Duck, Lady in Cement*); even Doctor Octopus himself Alfred Molina (*Boogie Nights, Pete's Meteor*) has put on the wax moustache in a TV version of *Murder on the Orient Express*, though without his huge metal tentacles! So, there we are, many different actors giving their own version of the same role; each with his own special qualities, each choosing to spotlight a different aspect of the character. **Who was the best?** It's impossible to say, and frankly that's not the object of the exercise. If pushed you'd probably say it was a **toss-up** between Ustinov and Suchet, but that's not the point. The point is that they all did a good job but they all **did it differently.**

It's the same with marriage! Different people do it differently! So what if Bob and Sue do things differently to you and Jane? Who cares? It doesn't matter.

Where it **does** matter is when the differences are not between different couples but between different people within **the same marriage**. Then you've got problems. Then we come back to my sub-heading:

Death on Denial

What do you mean by that, Keith? Why do you keep ranting on about Hercule Poirot? All right, let me explain.

1. You should know by now that I always explain my methods.

2. I'm not *ranting*, I'm reincorporating an earlier example, using repetition as a learning tool. Poirot is a universally known character, beloved the world over. He's a common denominator used here as a tool to bring readers together. If you can think of a better one then fine, go ahead and use it. Write your own book! It's not as easy as it looks, just getting this far has been really hard.

Denial. It's a popular word nowadays. What does it mean? The dictionary I consulted offers several definitions. I think definition four serves our purposes best: *a state of mind marked by a refusal or an inability to recognize and deal with a serious personal problem*. Bingo![1] A person is in denial if they refuse to see, recognize or deal with a serious personal problem. If they just pretend it isn't there, rather than face up to it, address it, deal with it and move on. Think of our old friend Lord Nelson, Yes, we have a column erected in his honour today; if you're planning a trip to London I recommend you visit it.[2] Not only was he famous for the Battle of the Nile, he was one of the first people on record to adopt the approach we now call "denial".

The Battle of Denial

"I see no ships!" he said as he held his telescope up to his bad eye. All right, technically yes, he *couldn't* see any ships, I'm not saying he could, but really the bad eye was no more

1 This (Bingo) is not the "serious personal problem" referred to in the dictionary definition. Certainly, if played to excess it could conceivably interfere with a person's day-to-day life, but as far as the author is aware there are no recorded cases of addiction. Bear in mind though that Bingo is in essence *gambling* and of course *gambling* can be highly addictive. Viewed in this light, Bingo can be seen as the tip of the iceberg and readers are therefore recommended to approach it with the utmost caution. Also, for the divorcee, Bingo brings its own set of problems. The traditional shouting of the word "House!" at the end of a game can be particularly upsetting and should be replaced by "bedsit", "flat" or "Dave's spare room".

2 Nelson's Column is in Trafalgar Square. Use Leicester Square Underground Station (Northern, Piccadilly Line).

than what we now call *a get-out clause*. He held the telescope up to his bad eye so that he could very craftily **be in denial and tell the truth at the same time!** In a relationship it's far more likely that when a person is in denial they are not telling the truth. They are using the denial as a way of **avoiding the truth**. I would never wish blindness on anyone, of course I wouldn't, but as you can see, sometimes it comes in handy.

So why did Nelson lie? Was it merely a blip, a "one off", a moment of madness? Or did it perhaps say something more about his deeper character? Well, he was a sailor of course and sailors are known to be huge liars. With a girl, and in these enlightened times often a boy, in every port, they have to be, for the sake of the smooth running of home and ship, inveterate liars; it's almost expected of them… ***"While the cat's away, the mice will play"***: we're all familiar with this phrase, well in this case it's the cat that's playing, while he's away at sea. Ironic really, given that cats are notoriously afraid of water! In all likelihood the mice are also playing, back on shore, and we find ourselves caught in a vicious circle of lies, deceit and infidelity, all because Lord Nelson, **one of the Greatest Britons of all time, was in denial**.

"What on earth has this got to do with my feelings of despondency, worthlessness and heartache?" OK, that's a fair question and it deserves a fair answer. Try a little experiment.

Experiment

1. Put on your special imaginary glasses.
2. Re-read my account of Lord Nelson and his telescope.
3. Picture yourself as Lord Nelson.
4. Instead of ships, imagine that you're looking for troubles on the horizon of your relationship.
5. Instead of a dicky eye, imagine that you're just *pretending* that you can't see any troubles.
6. Now, carry on "sailing".
7. Look out, there's cannon balls exploding all around me!
8. **That's right, you're sunk**.

There! Do you get my point? Just like Lord Nelson, **you're not facing up to the truth**. In your case it's not the lives of hundreds of men that are at risk (…and the odd woman. Films of the time often depict a young tomboyish stowaway, desperate to muck in with the men! She usually falls in love with one of them and then gets killed at the end.). **It's your marriage that's at risk** and rather than face up to the fact that things aren't all well at home, you sail on regardless. It's a futile action and typical of proud men who would rather pretend that everything's all right than admit there might be something wrong. So come on, look at your relationship and see if you can find any problems. If you're not currently in a relationship, and the chances are you're not, or you'd be reading a Grisham rather than a Barret, then think back to the glory days, pore over the past, rake it up and see if you can see where you went wrong. It's well worth doing. People say you shouldn't dwell on the past but I think it's a wonderful way of opening up your emotions. After all, without a past, there can be no future! Added to this, **we all feel better after a good cry**.

For the sake of the book, let's pretend that you **are** in a relationship. That's right! You! In a relationship! It sounds crazy, doesn't it? But it's not, it's excellent! It's nirvana! (The state of mind, not the pop group. If your relationship was like the Nirvana pop group it would be an awfully untidy thing where neither one of you could be bothered to make the bed.) You're living the dream that we all share. But wait, **is everything as it seems?** Are you really skating hand in hand on the temporary ice rink at Somerset House like John Cusack and the lovely Kate Beckinsale in that smashing video *Serendipity*? Or are you stomping your feet carelessly on very thin brittle ice in the middle of a freezing lake somewhere in the Deep South, like a special Christmas edition of *Deliverance*? Exactly! Things are often not as they seem. There must have been hundreds of men who thought that they were doing fine in their relationship, only to have the wool pulled over their eyes and the rug pulled from under their feet by the unhappy woman they'd thought was going to grow old with them. These men came a cropper because, like Lord Nelson, they refused to see the ships of discontent as they loomed on the horizon.

So what can we do, how can we hold our telescopes up to our good eyes and navigate round the enemy ships using only one hand? I don't know, but if you can pull it off, your lady will think you're the bees knees. I'm joking! I *do* know how and I'm going to share that information with you right now.

Trouble at Mill
(How to Spot When Things Aren't Right)

• As Sir Cliff said, "We Don't Talk Anymore". As always he was right. In my experience, when it comes to understanding what makes a relationship tick, you have to go a long way to better Sir Cliff!

• "The Sound of Silence" may have bought Art Garfunkel millions of dollars in songwriting fees, but in a relationship the sound of silence is deadly. One of the easiest signs to read when you are looking for trouble in a relationship is silence. With this in mind…

• Talk.

• Talk again.

- Keep talking.

- Even when she says, "Keith, I'm feeling tired, I've got a headache, I just need a little time to myself…" talk.

- If anything, that's the time to talk the most. It doesn't matter what you talk about, **just fill up those silences with chatter so she knows you're there**.

It's almost as though you're a spy! Constantly looking for clues as to the state of your relationship. Some of the clues are easy to see. A slap in the face, sudden tears and finding your partner in the arms of another are all fairly strong indicators of compatibility problems that even the most inept amateur detective can spot. However, **the more subtle clues are trickier to spot. An oddly placed pause** in an otherwise cheery conversation, **a peculiar look of disdain, an unusually long sigh, stinging criticism in front of friends and family**, surprisingly these too can be signs of problems in a relationship. At the same time of course they can also be just part and parcel of the day-to-day hustle and bustle. The oddly placed pause can just as easily be a pause for thought as your loved one's heart skips a beat as it can a pause to think, "What the hell am I doing with him?" The look of disdain can often be a simple reflex action caused by trapped wind, ditto the long sigh… The stinging criticism in front of friends and family is never nice, though, I must admit. But the other three, how can you accurately tell the feelings behind the actions? Well? "Come on Keith, how can you?" OK, I'm going to answer that question with three very important words, words that I want you to remember. **Words that form the cornerstone of what this book is all about**; words that I use again and again and that hopefully, when you've read this book, you will too.

I DON'T KNOW

There we are, three of the simplest words in the English language, coming together to form a vital phrase or saying to see you through the rocky path of life. These are words that will come to be like a security blanket to you as you navigate your way through the relationship maze. "I don't know, I don't know"… Try it now, say it to yourself under your breath. Once you allow these words to be your bible you will find a far greater sense of ease in so many areas.

Does this dress look good on me?

I DON'T KNOW

What shall we do tonight?

I DON'T KNOW

Have you emptied the dishwasher?

I DON'T KNOW

What the hell are you talking about?

I DON'T KNOW

I DON'T KNOW

I DON'T KNOW

I DON'T KNOW

I DON'T KNOW

I've left spaces above the last few for you to insert some of
the questions that mean the most to *you*. Take the time to
write them (in *pencil*, then you can rub them out ready for
new questions in your next relationship) then say them out
loud to yourself first thing in the morning, before you go

about your daily routine. Try this for a week or so and see how you feel. If you feel comfortable and ready, *and I must stress **only** if you feel comfortable and ready*, then you might want to move up to the next level.

Level 2

At Level 2, I've taken the three words forward to construct a small poem, mantra or chant (We're back in Paul McKenna territory!) which I think if anything is *even more* comforting than the question and answer arrangement. If you're one of those people who found poetry very difficult at school, don't worry, mine is awfully simple. Here we go:

Don't I know?
No I don't
I don't know...

Please feel free to use that poem on a daily basis, chant it quietly under your breath as you stroll down the high street, hop on the bus or listen to your partner's list of complaints. Then when the time is right, produce the final line as an end to all discussion/argument.

So, what have we learnt in this chapter? Probably the most important lesson I've wanted to pass on is that denial is a terrible thing and to be avoided at all costs. It stops you from being in touch with your real emotions, cuts you off from true feeling and creates an invisible barrier between you and your loved one. BUT if those true emotions are just too painful to deal with, we can always turn to our mantra for help.

I DON'T KNOW

Role-play

In this role-play, one of the most imaginative and challenging in the book, you get a chance to undergo a creative workout. To metaphorically speaking "stretch your wings and spread your legs". I've set it in the late 1700s, a time of great unrest, not just in England, but, as Lisa Stansfield might say, all around the world! You are Admiral Lord Horatio Nelson (see above), torn between the salty sea, Lady Hamilton and of course Fanny Nisbett. This role-play is an excellent exercise in both denial and choice, two issues that play a prominent role in any relationship; if played properly it can be a great help in distracting your mind from the pain of a failing marriage. Please don't be afraid of these exercises, thinking that they are not for you, that they are just for people who spend their afternoons playing Dungeons and Dragons and to a lesser extent Super Mario Bros. They're not, they're for everyone. By which I mean that if you **are** someone who spends his time playing Dungeons and Dragons then these exercises are for you too. Probably more so. Indeed if you are up to Level 6 on Dragon Slayer, the chances are that your relationship is in tatters as a direct result!

LADY HAMILTON It's no good, I can't carry on like this, seeing you behind the back of my husband Lord Hamilton. It's just not right!

LORD NELSON I know.

LADY HAMILTON And you're never here!

LORD NELSON I know.

LADY HAMILTON Things have come to a head. I want you to stop sailing, leave Fanny Nisbett and make a decent woman out of me...

Things are obviously coming to a head and it's vital that you act decisively. How do you respond? Do you...

A: Turn your back on your sailor friends? (Choice)

B: Tell her that you "see no problems" (Denial)

C: Apologize and hold her in your arm (Reconciliation)

Again, I don't know which choice you've made, but in the spirit of the rest of the book I hope it's the right one. Good Luck!

NOW I KNOW

✱ There are as many different ways of making a successful marriage as there are colours of doors.

✱ Our differences make us special.

✱ They can sometimes cause us pain.

✱ David and John Suchet are brothers.

✱ Viewing your relationship as a "dead cat" is unhealthy.

✱ Paul McKenna is a mystical man.

4

Share the Blame

Share the Shame

"Blame it on the Sun"

STEVIE WONDER – BLAME IT ON THE SUN

"Blame it on Rio"

MICHAEL CAINE – BLAME IT ON RIO

"It wasn't me"

SHAGGY FEAT, RIKROK – IT WASN'T ME

We live in an age of blame. "Whose fault is it?" That's a question we hear more and more. Everyone is unhappy with his or her lot and so they want to blame someone; some blame the government; some even blame their parents. Michael Jackson, of course, once saw fit to Blame it on the Boogie. It's interesting to note that during his recent troubles he seems to have changed horses midstream and focused his attention on the media, saying they were to blame, with no mention being made of the Boogie, which appears to have got away scot free along with the Sunshine, the Moonlight and the Good Times who had all at some point felt the **full glare of the finger of suspicion**.

While we're on legal matters it's worth noting the enormous number of television adverts these days that promise a "no win, no fee" court case. Not the actual number. I once tried a quick Google on that figure but came up empty handed; admittedly the computer I was using, owned by Hounslow Council and part of its library services, had its Parental Controls option ticked in System Preferences so that may have had some bearing on the rather limited outcome. The Parental Control had been set by the previous librarian and when she left she took the password with her, much to the annoyance of the new librarian, Jayne, with a "Y". I've just realized, there's no need to say "with a Y" when you're writing it down! Anyway, it was much to the annoyance of Jayne, with a "Y", the new librarian who is a lovely lady. As she whispered to me, "Keith, I've tried to guess it so many times, I'm at my wit's end." We had a crack at it together one wet afternoon; I asked Jayne a range of questions about her predecessor, in an effort to build up a psychological profile, **to get inside her mind**. Her name, I quickly discovered, was Ruth Cooper, née Slate, a happily married Taurean originally from Totnes in Devon, who had left the Library on retirement when she and her husband David moved lock, stock and barrel (That was a smashing video! I look forward to his next one...) to Cyprus for his legs. Over the course of the afternoon I was to learn a lot more about Ruth and David, but nothing that I felt could unlock the password, until quite by chance an elderly lady came to the desk to take out a copy of *The Silent World of Nicholas Quinn*, by Colin Dexter, one of the *Inspector Morse* series, and Jayne remarked that Ruth had been a huge fan of *Inspector Morse*. Eureka! I pointed out that people often base their passwords around their favourite things so with no time to spare we spent a few hours trying various Morse-related words. We started with "Morse"... no luck. "Inspector"... ditto. "Lewis"... no. "Jaguar" (the car, not the animal)... nope. Undeterred I continued to wrack my brain. Then it came to me! A password is a *secret*. What was Inspector Morse's secret? That's right, his Christian name… Endeavour! We could barely type straight with excitement, slowly and with huge grins across our faces, I tapped out the letters, **E N D E A V O U R …**

Nothing. But I refuse to look defeat in the face; I had one further trick up my sleeve. I went back and re-entered all the words, but this time in lower case.

Again, nothing. To say that this broke our spirit would be accurate. We tried a few more – "Thaw", "Whately", "Repeat" – but it was no use, so we admitted defeat. I could see how much this upset Jayne. She had told me in previous chats that she **sometimes suffered from depression**; nothing too heavy, just a general down in the dumps, no point in getting out of bed, "Why are we all here?" kind of thing. Although, by her own admission, she had been hospitalized in the mid-nineties. I say "by her own admission" in as much as she told me this of her own free will. Funnily enough the hospitalization itself was quite the opposite. "Keith, they had to drag me kicking and screaming", she'd quietly told me one February morning. It was a dreadful affair and in all honesty, when the subject comes up these days I try to distract her, so sensing that we might be strolling down memory lane I quickly grabbed the nearest book to hand and presented it to her, with my ticket on top, ready to borrow, so that she might feel that she had a purpose in life. It was lying face down, a big hefty old book, hardback, which I calculated to probably be an historical work, possibly on Hitler or maybe Nazis in general, Jayne says they fly off the shelves… Imagine my surprise when I turned it over and found it to be a biography of The Bee Gees! It was huge, in many ways it seemed too big for a pop biography, but I suppose when you think about it, it's actually three biographies in one, one for each brother. Saying that, the author devotes a surprising amount of time to Andy, the fourth Bee Gee, so that can't help. I don't mean to be cruel in saying "a surprising amount of time", it's just that I hadn't realized how big Andy was. Like most of us, I'd never really seen beyond Barry, Robin and Maurice. But Andy was very big in America, he went out with Victoria Principal from *Dallas*, and was in the stage show of *The Pirates of Penzance*, long before the film with Johnny Depp and Gareth from *The Office*. The book itself is exhaustive, meticulously researched and in terms of punctuation, faultless. It's a few years old now and so ends on a high note (I know what you're thinking! "Just like their songs!" And you'd be right, up to a point…)

Barry's **distinctive falsetto**, which we now think of as "the Bee Gee sound", in fact **only came about in the mid seventies** when the brothers were hard at work in the studio laying down *Nights on Broadway*… "*Blaming it all, on those nights on Broadway*…" There we are, back to blame! Producer Arif Mardin asked if one of the boys, he didn't specify who, could come out with a high-pitched riff towards the end of the "track". Step forward, not surprisingly, Barry. He's the elder brother, the unofficial leader and a good friend of

Barbra Streisand, who let rip with the sound that would go on to earn the lucky brothers **hundreds of pounds around the world**. Before this, on songs like "Massachusetts", "Words" (later covered by Boyzone) and "New York Mining Disaster", the Bee Gees sound quite normal. Incidentally, if you're wondering where you've seen the name Arif Mardin before, he went on to produce the very popular album, *Come Away With Me* by Norah Jones. Norah sounds Welsh but in fact she isn't. She's the daughter of one of the best sitar players in the world, Ravi Shankar.[1]

Anyway, the book came out a few years ago and so luckily ends before the death of Maurice, a very sad event, not just for Barry and Robin, but for the whole Gibb family and not something to be discussed in a book like this.

---

1 If she were Welsh, she could be the daughter of course of our own Sitar King, *Tom Jones*; mind you, if he'd been involved the album would probably have been called *Come Away With Me… for a bit of you know what*! I'm only joking, of course I am. It's a bit of fun.

Whose Fault Is It?

"We all have our faults, mine's in California."

LEX LUTHOR – *SUPERMAN 1*

The fault that Lex was referring to of course was the San Andreas Fault in California and his dastardly plan to fire highjacked missiles into The Fault, sending miles of coastal California into the sea, leaving behind a new coastline, made up of land that he'd recently purchased for next to nothing, which he planned to sell on at a hugely inflated price. **A truly abhorrent act and in this age of gazumping chillingly plausible**. Luckily Superman flew around the world backwards, causing time to reverse, foiled his plan, sending the missiles back to their launchers and saving the life of Lois Lane.

I have to say that a lot of Superman fans, myself included, see this "turning back time" as a bit of a Get out of Jail Free Card. Why doesn't he just do it every time, even for the slightest misdemeanour? It's just too easy and spoils an otherwise enjoyable franchise. Also it's very difficult to watch a keen, agile Christopher Reeve in the first film, knowing the dreadful turn of events that were just around the corner. I'm talking of course about *Superman IV*, *The Quest For Peace*, an absolute travesty of a fantasy feature, with The Man of Steel pitted against Nuclear Man in an ill-thought-through metaphor for East–West Cold War tensions. Frankly, this sort of **knee-jerk posturing** is better left to the more politically aware actors like Jane Fonda, Spike Lee and more recently Sylvester Stallone who in *Rocky V* summed up the hopes and fears of a generation as he took on the formidable Russian heavyweight Ivan Drago. Rocky won of course but it was touch and go right up to the final moments.

So what can we learn from this? Well, the lesson comes, somewhat surprisingly, from Lex Luthor himself. When he says, "We all have our faults," he's being honest, he's opening up, admitting that he's not perfect. It's an admirable quality in anyone, this willingness to criticize oneself, and the fact that it comes from Lex makes it doubly impressive. So come on! If the greatest criminal mind of our times can admit that he falls short in some areas, then surely **so can you!** This admission is one of the two cornerstones of any relationship and the perfect soil for planting the foundations of trust and growth. **Being able to admit that you are not perfect is the first step toward recognizing that other people have faults and imperfections too, and understanding that this just makes them human, like you**.

I will say on balance that this is where Lex falls down. In spite of being able to recognize his own weaknesses he has remained **criminally intolerant of shortcomings in others** and remains **a threat to the civilized world**. He must be stopped; Superman, where are you?!

It's a bit of fun.

"Blame By Any Other Name…"

As we've established earlier in the book, it's a fact of modern-day life that blame is bandied about all over the place; but what exactly do we mean by the word "blame"? Well, the dictionary tells us this:

blame:

1. to consider somebody to be responsible for something wrong or unfortunate that has happened   2. to find fault with somebody.

That's what the dictionary says and the dictionary must be right, right?

WRONG!

I think that the word blame is often misused… Actually, as I write this I realize that I am about to argue against myself! I've got myself in a bit of a twist… What I want to say is not that I disagree with the dictionary definition of a word; that would be madness; but that I don't think "blame" is the right word to use when talking about a divorce. Sorry, I went off on a tangent there and almost made a fool of myself. What I meant to say is that when you're talking about divorce, surely the word "credit" is a better one than "divorce".

A good divorce is like a fine wine, it gets better with age and is a credit to the family from which it comes.

A vintner would never shy away from taking credit for a fine wine and neither should you from taking credit for your divorce. The problem is that a society has grown up where the word "blame" is used instead of "credit" when referring to something negative; well, if we've learnt anything from this book it's that divorce needn't be negative. It's time to use the power of Word Switching (Fig. 10) again to steer us through these choppy waters.

Fig. 10

BLAME

CREDIT

By applying the Word Switching technique we are able to view divorce in a **new, better and more constructive light**. Now that we've turned it into a good word, why not share it around a bit? "Credit where credit's due" is an excellent phrase to turn to at this time, it makes a lot of sense and sounds much better than "blame where blame's due" which has a dreadful ring of negativity to it. So when you think of the breakdown of your marriage (or break-up, that works too... Is the glass half full or half empty? "I don't know, but whatever it is, darling, please don't throw it at me again!" It's a bit of fun.) You should be willing to spread the credit to all involved parties and *yes* that means the children too.[1]

---

1 See Step 5, "Why *Not* in Front of the Children? Letting the Little Ones Play Their Part.

For a divorce to really fly, you should encourage everyone to feel responsible for what's happened, so that everyone can take credit: husband, wife, children, in-laws, etc., they're all in it up to their necks! Don't for example feel that you can't talk to your partner's parents, what I call the "in-laws". If they've heard that your marriage is falling apart at the seams they are going to want to know why this is happening, what's been going on. Or as they themselves might say, "What the bleeping bleep has been going on?" If this is the case then please tell them what they need to hear, open up to them, go into detail, you'll be surprised how comfortable they are with revelations that you might previously have thought of as being too intimate. They'll have heard far worse on Trisha!

Make a List

Now that we've recognized that no one is perfect, we can move forward towards a more harmonious life with those around us. But first we need to ask some big questions.

1. Why am I not perfect?

2. What is not perfect about me?

3. What are my imperfections?

4. Can I perfect my imperfections?

These questions are all variations on a theme and essentially ask the same single question, "What are my imperfections?" I've stretched them out into four separate questions to show how important it is to make lists. Lists can be a great help to us in this modern world where life flies by at a terrific pace, they are nature's pauses, a chance to slow down. In answering this list of questions I suggest that you compile another list; in fact another two lists…

WHAT'S WRONG WITH ME

Be the Best... Not!

There is great pressure in society at the moment for the individual to be the best. We all remember Wham! shooting straight to the top of the charts with their hit record "Young Guns" and the frenetic dance routine that accompanied it on *Top of the Pops*, two young men (and their friends Pepsi and Shirley) living life to the full, enjoying every moment of their

---

WHAT'S WRONG WITH HIM/HER

_____

_____

_____

_____

_____

_____

_____

_____

_____

_____

_____

_____

_____

_____

_____

crazy, leather-jacketed and cap, sleeved, T-shirted youth; and why not? It was a bit of fun! How many of us, though, remember the title of that song in full? Not just "Young Guns", but "Young Guns, Go For It!" **"Go For It!"**; it's a potent piece of lingo, but what exactly does it mean? Go for what exactly? I think what they're saying is, "Go for the top", "the top of the heap", "the big cheese", "numero uno". All well and good, but the thing is **there's only room for one at the top**, so what happens to all the rest? Must they all be considered losers? In a way, yes, they must; in the sense of facing up to the fact that they didn't quite make it to the top, there's no getting away from it; only a fool would say otherwise, but in another way, no.

Exercise 1

Take a look at this list I've made of some of the great songs of our time. Read it slowly, taking in all the words as they appear on the page; when you've done that, read it again.

- "Brown Sugar" –The Rolling Stones
- "Strawberry Fields Forever" – The Beatles
- "Wonderwall" – The Oasis
- "Rocket Man" – Elton John
- "Bootylicious" – Destiny's Child
- "Suspicious Minds" – Elvis Presley
- "Torn" – Natalie Imbruglia
- "Vienna" – Ultravox

What a list! What a collection! What a shame!

Wait a minute, Keith, what do you mean by "What a shame"? It's a cracking collection of **timeless classics**, what on earth are you talking about? OK, I'll explain… Take another look at the list of songs (that's right, you should now be on your third look), they all have one thing in common, and it's something that they're not too happy about. Have you guessed? That's right! **None of them got to number one in the pop charts**; it's a collection of number twos. All of the songs peaked at number two and had to sit and watch in frustration as another song went to the top spot.

Particularly frustrating for Ultravox as their moustachioed, fund-raising lead singer "Midge" Ure had to bow to the musical superiority of The Joe Dolce Music Orchestra and "Shaddup Your Face!" Imagine that! Let's hope that time has softened the blow for Midge and that now he can look back and say, "It means nothing to me…"

It's a bit of fun!

Here's my point:

The fact that these lovely songs were number twos and yet we still all think they're great shows that there's nothing to be ashamed of in coming second.

When a marriage ends, the person left behind can often feel like the number two song in the charts and that's not a nice feeling, but as my list shows, sometimes **the number two is**

better than the number one. That's not always the case though; take a look at **this** list…

Exercise 2

- "Unchained Melody" – Robson and Jerome
- "My Sweet Lord" – George Harrison
- "I Don't Want to Talk About It" – Rod Stewart

All the above songs were number ones; here are the tracks that they held off the top spot…

- "Common People" – Pulp
- "Get the Party Started" – Pink
- "God Save the Queen" – The Sex Pistols

Here we can see that sometimes a number one is a number one for good reason: *it's a better song*. Likewise with marriage, and it's important to know, when you're a number two, that sometimes you have to step aside for a better song. Or man. Is this a pessimistic view? Maybe. Is the glass half full or half empty? Many would rush to say it's half full, and who could blame them? I say that **sometimes it *is* half empty**, and that's fine, **there's less chance of spilling it!**

If Music Be the Food of Love…

Music is a wonderful analogy for love and relationships; let's explore it further. As far as I can tell, in the old days number ones and relationships had one thing in common: **they both lasted longer**. I'm thinking in particular of Wet, Wet, Wet and Bryan Adams, both of these titans had huge number ones, which like a good marriage lasted for ages. The late Freddie Mercury, for example, stayed at number one for nine weeks with his "Bohemian Rhapsody"; in marriage terms this can't be far off a Ruby Wedding! Ironically and rather sadly, of course, Freddie's own romantic life was characterized by a series of tawdry, sordid, fleeting encounters that have come to typify the lifestyle of the predatory homosexual.

It's a bit of fun!

See, also, how people's record buying habits have changed over the years. In the past a person would find himself or herself attracted to a band, make a commitment and then stay with them through thick and thin; as an example let's look at Duran Duran. A real fan of these New Romantic renegades would have stuck with them come what may, from the giddy heights of a "Rio" or a "Girls on Film" to the depths of that ridiculous, far-fetched song about a union for snakes. An individual moment of pop madness wouldn't matter; the fan had made a commitment and intended to honour it. Nowadays, of course, bands are manufactured and then destroyed in the blink of an eye, Hear'Say, Steps, S Club 7, all fleeting affairs, the relationship equivalent of a one-night stand, or at best a series of passion-filled encounters that fizzles out after two to three weeks.

The same thing seems to have happened with relationships: in the past they were built to last, Cilla Black, Ronnie Corbett, Thora Hird… Nowadays we are constantly reminded of the transitory nature of human relationships. Nowhere is this more the case than in the **topsy-turvy world of show business**; some of our biggest stars whose unions seemed to be cast in stone have in recent years come unstuck. I'm thinking in particular of two very bright stars, Jade Goody and Jeff Brazier whose coming together united the nation in a way we'd not seen since the wedding of Prince Charles and Lady Diana Spencer. When word got out that the talented two-some were together, I would have sworn that the mood of the nation lifted. Even the pigeons seemed to have a spring in their step. It seemed too good to be true. It was. They came unstuck. Why? Who's to blame? Is it about blame? I think it is. "OK Keith, these are big words you're bandying about. Who exactly are you blaming? Put your money where your mouth is…" Fine, I will, and if this means that the book isn't reviewed favourably then so be it!

THE MEDIA

That's right, I blame the media! With their long lenses and even longer pens, they pry their way into people's lives without a care for the damage they cause. Look what they did to Jade and Jeff:

- They pursued the couple relentlessly.

- Whether it was the opening of a film, restaurant or night-club, it didn't matter, the media were there.

- Since leaving the Big Brother house together, Jade and Jeff had done some great work: the exercise video, *Celebrity Wife Swap*, the list goes on.

- But it wasn't enough for the media, they wouldn't focus on the work. Why, oh why not?

- Like Velociraptors in *Jurassic Park* or *Jurassic Park II* (by which time the scaly predators had, if anything, become even more vindictive…) they (the media) stalked our couple mercilessly.

- Constantly probed and undermined, there was only one way the relationship could go.

- Split.

- Jeff and Jade lose out.

- Their families lose out.

- We the public lose out. *Celebrity Wife Swap 2*? "Yes please!" Sorry, no!

- Who wins?

THE MEDIA

NOW I KNOW

* Everybody blames somebody.

* A good divorce is like a fine wine.

* Admitting you're not perfect is OK.

* "Strawberry Fields Forever" didn't get to number one.

5

Why *Not* in Front of the Children?

Letting the Little Ones Play Their Part

"You're having my baby…"

PAUL ANKA – YOU'RE HAVING MY BABY

"I believe that children are the future"

WHITNEY HOUSTON – THE GREATEST LOVE OF ALL

"Did you think I would leave you crying?"

ROLF HARRIS – TWO LITTLE BOYS

Many warring couples say that they stay together for the children; despite huge rows and open hostility between partners, they hang on together for the sake of the little ones. I think **this is a great idea** and I for one heartily recommend it. It is my considered opinion that we underestimate children and the extent to which they wrap themselves up in their own little child-like worlds, oblivious to what's going on around them.

I would go further than that and urge you to include them; in a house becalmed in the eerie silence of a post-row lull, who better to ferry notes between the tight-lipped warring parties? That's right, the kids! Make it fun!

Write your notes on coloured paper and send the children around the house on their trikes and bikes like couriers.[1]

Scuttling around the hallway on their skateboards and roller skates just like their heroes in *The Starlight Express*. This **makes them feel involved** and part of the peace-making process, like scaled-down Kofi Annans. If, like most children nowadays, they love to watch the soap operas then they'll know only too well that family life is no bed of roses and that loud, aggressive, upsetting arguments are part and parcel of the rough and tumble of the day to day. By seeing you and your loved one fighting, it'll make them feel like they're in *Emmerdale*, or better still *EastEnders*; something every child dreams of! There are steps you and you're your loved one can take to help your little smashers along the way with this fantasy:

1. As you argue, shout, "Leave it out!" in a loud, aggressive manner.

2. When the row is over, tell the children that it's "sorted". They'll love it.

1 Ironically, Dr David Cowley, in his paper "Broken Home, Broken Child", states that a high percentage of children from homes in which both parents are not present will often find themselves working in low-level manual work such as couriers in later life.

3. Why not rig up a video camera and let the children film your rows? In this age of *Big Brother* and *Celebrity Driving School*, it'll make them feel like they're working in the world of television and maybe point them in the right direction for a future career. Also, should things reach the courts, you'll both have a reliable record of who said what to whom. Bang, everyone's happy!

It's a Dog's Life...

When a relationship goes south, by which I mean goes wrong as opposed to relocating to Cornwall which can in fact be beneficial to a relationship on many levels, not least in terms of an all-round healthier lifestyle, and easy access to a wide range of organically grown farmhouse produce, it's assumed that high on the list of casualties will be the kids or "children". As adults we are told to protect our children from being exposed to things that we feel might harm them, things that we remember from our own childhood that we suspect hindered our own progress.

Hmm... I'm not so sure. Allow me to challenge conventional wisdom once again!

Case Study

In this particular case study we will examine the story of a randomly chosen individual, Person "A". Person "A", a kind and loving father from Wales, spent a lot of time with his little smashers, "R" and "A", trying to steer them away from any examples of cruelty to animals, for fear of it having an ill effect on their young impressionable psyches. As a child himself, he had the misfortune to witness the dreadful sight of a demented dog spinning round and round chasing his own tail. It was at Gareth Morris's house one Easter, for his thirteenth birthday party, and all the children were in the garden with their eggs. Gareth thought it would be funny to put chocolate on Bodie's tail and see what happened. Bodie, a Border Collie named after Lewis Collins's cocksure detective in ITV's answer to *Starsky and Hutch*, *The Professionals*, was recovering from a recent stomach operation for dogs and still slightly woozy from the anaesthetic but somehow managed to actually catch his own tail. I know! In normal circumstances this would have been cause for celebration, but not this time. The anaesthetic still present in his dog body meant that Bodie had no feeling in his farthest extremity and so proceeded to eat his own tail! It was a sickening, outrageous act and one that has stayed with Person "A" well into adulthood. To this day he is still unable to stroke a dog any further than the midsection of his or her back; I'm sorry to say that **the same is true of cats**.

Of course, Gareth Morris thought it was hilarious and rolled around on the grass in hysterics. His mother though took a different view and in a beautifully judged act of diplomacy cancelled a planned game of "Pin the Tail on the Donkey" in protest. Gareth's response to this was to go berserk; he swept his outstretched arms across the dinner table, sending a **huge**

home-made raspberry trifle crashing to the floor, and then had to be forcibly restrained by his older brother Lee, assuming the paternal role in the absence of their Dad, still at the vet's with the injured Bodie. Gareth was later diagnosed as having **Attention Deficit Disorder** or ADD and was pre-scribed the controversial drug Ritalin, which had no effect whatsoever. If anything he became even *more* anti-social and within a year his parents had split up; Gareth went and lived with his father in Newport while Lee stayed with his mother and her sister. Then on his sixteenth birthday Gareth announced that he was gay! I know, unbelievable! This was ter-ribly upsetting for his father Ray, who had always been very Welsh and wasted no time in throwing Gareth out of the house.

A terrible chain of events that started with an upsetting image of an animal in distress; only a fool would suggest that events were related but I think that **there could be a link**.

The point I'm making is that for a young mind to witness animal cruelty can be very upsetting, but that needn't be a bad thing. **What better way to grow up into sensi-tive, animal-friendly men than to witness extreme acts of gore at a young age?**

Case Study

In another example, Person "A" and his ex-wife (though they were married at the time, happily so, as far as he was concerned) once took their little smashers to a zoo in Majorca. It was a baking hot day with little or no shade and they trudged wearily around, peering into dusty enclosures at the poor skinny undernourished creatures inside. People make a great fuss about the awful conditions in continental zoos and I think they're right. The café at this one was outdoor, the drinks came out of a box, not a fridge, and we had to sit with our food under direct sunlight as the only shade was taken by a small group of Spanish youths who despite the heat had their hoods up and their jeans half way down their bottoms.

They (Person "A" and his wife) had almost finished their tour when "A" (not Person "A", but the child of Person "A", whose name just happens to start with "A"; let's call him Alyn) made a beeline for the monkeys, running as fast as his little sunburned legs could carry him; he eventually stopped dead, just short of the cage, and stood transfixed. When his parents finally caught up with him they were shocked to see that the little monkey was actually masturbating. It was three o'clock in the afternoon. They arrived just at the moment of climax; "A" had witnessed it all while "R" just caught the tail end. **It was appalling**.

But, and it's a big but, the incident has in no way impaired their enjoyment of our simian cousins. They still get a kick out of King Louie as he exposes counterfeit monkey Baloo the Bear in Rudyard Kipling's wonderful animation, *The Jungle Book*. They experience no Vietnam-style flashback horrors when playing at the park on the monkey bars; and I'm told that modern director and partner of Helena Bonham-Carter, Tim Burton's re-imagining of the classic *Planet of the Apes* is rarely out of the DVD player!

So, if a frenetic cannibalistic dog and a self-pleasuring monkey do no harm, then believe me, seeing Mum and Dad enduring three months of silence, exchanging poisonous glances, shouting at each other, running up the stairs in tears, throwing crockery at each other, hurling clothes out of a bedroom window and charging at each other with cutlery is barely going to make a scratch on their young tender psyches.

IF ANYTHING IT WILL TOUGHEN THEM UP.

And three cheers for that!

All together now, "Sorted!"

The Great Divide

The problems of maintaining a healthy male/female relationship are as perplexing and relevant today as they've ever been; it's an issue that has vexed society from the outset. The sexes seem destined to be forever at odds with each other;

my friend Paul Lucas put it nicely when he said that probably, when man invented fire, a woman straight away complained that it was too hot!

A bit unfair but it does illustrate the point in an accessible way through the use of humour. In all honesty it's quite tame coming from Paul, he's had terrible luck with the ladies and harbours quite a grudge. I said that to him once that he "harboured quite a grudge" and quick as a flash he snapped back, "I haven't got a boat!" Ouch! That sort of quick-fire

humour is perfect on a show like *Have I Got News For You*, or the slightly ruder *They Think It's All Over Now*, but in an intimate relationship it can cause offence and hurt. There aren't many women who can put up with that kind of ribbing on a daily basis, Gaby Roslin springs to mind, but even she's gone quiet lately. The thing is that when it comes to men and women, we're just different; it's as simple as that.

As the author John Gray says in his book, *Men Are From Mars, Women Are From Venus*, "Men are from Mars, women are from Venus", and while he doesn't mean for us to take that literally, he makes the point that we have our differences; although the distance **doesn't** have to be that great (in John's case, interplanetary) for differences to emerge. My friends David Price and Gillian Cole had one of the worst marriages on record, going at each other hammer and tongs, often in front of friends, until finally divorcing just before Christmas last year. Their families were heartbroken and the small dry cleaning business they had built up had to be sold off. They didn't hail from two different planets, they came from Porthcawl and Bridgend respectively. Two South Wales towns in very close proximity and well served by local transport. So be warned, coming from the same area is no guarantee of a long, happy marriage, in many cases it can make it worse. One of the problems with David and Gillian was David's endless probing of his wife and her moods. He was constantly asking her how she was, how she was feeling, etc., and this got on her pip no end. As she herself once said to me at the famous Halloween Party of 2001, an evening memorable for many things, not least Carol Ball arriving dressed as Michael Jackson from his *Thriller* period, as Gillian said to me, "Keith, I wish he'd stop. If he doesn't then I don't see any future for this marriage." I took that as a sign that all was not well in the marriage and time has, regrettably, proven me right. The lesson to be learned is that **there is nothing to be gained from poking and prodding your partner**, trying to understand them. For men this is a pointless task, so don't bother. **It's like trying to predict the tides**.

What Are You Talking About?

"Communication let me down"

SPANDAU BALLET – COMMUNICATION

So sang Tony Hadley and his friends in Spandau Ballet, way back in February of 1983. It is as strong a message now as it was then. Time has done nothing to diminish its impact. Communication *can* let us down; from poor reception on a mobile phone to a basic lack of understanding between men and women or gay couples, **it's vitally important that we communicate clearly if we are to thrive**.

As always, it's not *what* you say but *how* you say it that matters; Hadley understood this, so did those other musical firebrands The Fun Boy Three when they enlisted the help of The Bananarama in February of 1982 for their hit "It Ain't What You Do It's The Way That You Do It". It's not *what* we say; it's *how* we say it! So come on, smile!

That's right, it's as simple as that, a smile can make all the difference. When Glasgow, a city for years associated with deprivation, drunkenness and violence was made European City of Culture in 1990, their slogan was "Glasgow's Miles Better". Try saying it! That's right, it sounds like, "Glasgow Smiles Better", in an instant sweeping away the enduring image of Glasgow as a hotbed of urban deprivation, organized crime and alcohol and drug-related problems. In its place came a lovely image of a whole Scottish city smiling. While on one

level it wasn't fooling anyone, it did none the less send out a strong message of happiness and soon when we thought of Glasgow we thought of smiles.

A doctor friend of mine once informed me that it takes forty-three muscles to frown but only seventeen to smile. Incredible! Medical proof that it's harder to feel sad than it is to feel happy, yet very few people know just how powerful a smile can be. As we look around us, with the exception of female weather presenters like the lovely Sian Lloyd, smiles can be hard to come by. That's a shame, because in the right hands, or mouths, **a smile can be a potent tool**.

Politicians know this; we are very fortunate in Great Britain to have in Tony Blair a Prime Minister with one of the nicest smiles this country has ever seen, and across the pond, George W. Bush always manages a little grin, even on the gravest of occasions. His "We'll smoke them out!" speech could have been very upsetting were it not for that infectious, cheeky and in many ways almost *inappropriate* little smirk that's never far from his Texan lips.

When that other George, George Michael, was told he was gay, he didn't hide himself away, wrapped up with guilt and shame, instead he went on the Parkinson Show with a spring in his step and a huge smile on his face, like the cat that's got the cream, and duly confounded his critics. As he himself would say, "I think that's amazing!"[1]

It all shows the power of the smile. This can work in print as well as with the spoken word; let's try an experiment.

1 "Amazing" – George Michael, from the CD *Patience*, Sony Music UK 5054022000. Parental Guidance, Explicit Lyrics. While on the show, George performed a lovely, live version of "A Different Corner" which is available on the CD of his hit single "As", the Stevie Wonder song, performed here as a duet with Mary J. Blige.

Experiment

AUNTY JEAN HAS DIED.

"Aunty Jean has died" – a terrible statement, awful, shocking… the last thing any of us wanted to hear. We don't know the cause of her death and it doesn't matter, we know that she's dead and that's enough, it's bad news.

But wait a minute; what if Aunty Jean had been suffering from a terrible disease for many years, unable to interact with her family and loved ones? Ending up just a drain, physically, financially and emotionally, on her long-suffering, duty-bound family. Then maybe, just maybe, her death would be a **blessed relief**, still news but now *good* news. You might even say it with a smile. Have a try: imagine that Aunty Jean has died and that you're telling the assembled family who are waiting, huddled around a vending machine in the hospital corridor, the news. First try it with a straight face: "Aunty Jean has died." Hmm, not very nice at all, is it? Now try it with a smile: "Aunty Jean has died!" "Aunty Jean has died!" What did you notice? That's right, it doesn't seem so bad! Now, if a smile can add an element of fun to the death of a much-loved family member then just think what it can do in ordinary everyday life, how it can make things better. Don't believe me? Watch this:

Aunty Jean has died.

Exactly! All I did was change the font; up from 11 to 22 and from Cheltenham to Matrix script and suddenly it looks like a celebration. The message is clear: *Change your font*, and your life will turn around.

"In other words…"
FRANK SINATRA – FLY ME TO THE MOON

In April of 1983 F.R. David said, "Words don't come easy," and he had a point although I think he would have been more on the button if he'd said, "*The right* words don't come easy." Words, after all, are all around us, everywhere we look, indeed only two years earlier The Tom Tom Club, in "Wordy Rappinghood", said (or rapped!):

> **"Eat your words**
> **but don't go hungry,**
> **words have always nearly hung me."**

The Tom Tom Club showed an eerie understanding of the potency of language. They knew the awesome power of words and how they can help to lift or lower our spirits depending on how we choose to choose them. For example, elsewhere in this book I analyse suicide rates in the UK. It's not an easy read, I readily admit. I labelled the charts I compiled thus: SUICIDE SINCE 1990. It was direct, to the point, functional, stark almost.

SUICIDE

Since 1990

Scotland 17%	**INCREASE**
Northern Ireland 10%	**INCREASE**
Rep. Ireland 8%	**INCREASE**
England 6%	**DECREASE**

Wales 7% DECREASE!

To borrow from one of my favourite TV adverts, it "did exactly what it says on the tin!" In choosing that label though I may have lost some readers who felt that it was a subject on which they didn't wish to dwell. OK, that's fine; it would be odd if it were any different, if the thought of the UK's suicide rates got you all fired up! As strange as it may seem, there *are* people like that. I once saw a documentary on Bravo about a man who could only make love if he thought about taking his own life, so hey ho, horses for courses. Indeed, later that night on Bravo+1, so technically it had first been broadcast an hour earlier, was a documentary along a similar theme about a man and his horse... Appalling!

Anyway, a little later in the section I referred to suicide as "doing something silly", a very common saying, a phrase that we are all familiar with. Now then, what if I'd labelled my chart that way? What effect might it have had? Let's try…

DOING SOMETHING SILLY

Since 1990

Scotland	**17%**	**INCREASE**
Northern Ireland	**10%**	**INCREASE**
Rep. Ireland	**8%**	**INCREASE**
England	**6%**	**DECREASE**

Wales 7% DECREASE!

There, now it's turned around 360 degrees. It's still the same information, the same savage indictment of mental health in Blair's Britain but it's much more accessible, almost appealing, and it's all happened by simply choosing different words. So, what has this got to do with relationships? Everything, it has everything to do with relationships and it doesn't matter whether you're a heterosexual or a homosexual, gay or straight, whichever side of the coin you fall on. You have to communicate!

I'm Bored!

Many modern couples, when asked why they had an affair or split up, say "I was bored"! Personally, I'm never bored, there's always something to look at. Life is a big book, and I can't put it down! But just because I'm never bored, it doesn't mean that I can't appreciate what it's like for **people that are**. It isn't nice.

What do we mean by "bored"? Well, for me it's quite difficult to put it into words; if pushed I suppose I would say that it's **a general lack of interest in what's going on around me, a listlessness coupled with a lack of energy, a sort of lethargy combined with a feeling of the grass being greener in the other man's garden and a creeping sense of depression. Sometimes it's almost a physical ache that saps the very life force from your veins and pulls you down deeper and deeper until you feel the earth closing in around you and filling your ears and mouth with dirt and worms.**

This is fine if it's just something in yourself, but what if it's your partner? Disaster! For a relationship to flourish, we must always be checking on our partners and making sure that they are not bored. There are many ways to do this. Speaking personally, during my marriage I was rarely bored and for that

I have to thank my wife, Marion. When I was lucky enough to be at home with my little smashers, Marion made sure that I had plenty to do in the form of little notes left around the home. You may have read about this kind of thing before: sweet nothings written on scented sheets of coloured paper pledging eternal love, declarations of undying devotion, that sort of thing… But not Marion, she's a practical woman and knew only too well that that sort of note would only leave me moping and pining for her; if anything it would make me miss her more. No, she would leave little jobs to be done round the house, ironing, hoovering, window cleaning, that sort of thing. Put that together with looking after two growing boys and I simply didn't have time to be bored!

So what can you do to keep the travelling salesman of boredom away from the front door of your partner's mind?[1]

There are many ways to keep your partner amused…

- Poetry: Write her a poem, read her a poem.
- Silly notes.
- Flowers.

But what about you? Use the space at the bottom of this page to list all the things that you do.

1 That's nice, isn't it? I think the writing is coming on leaps and bounds as the book progresses.

Look Around You!

If you are feeling bored and a little sorry for yourself, one of the best things to do is to go back to bed, pull the covers right over your head and wait for the feeling to pass. Fine, but what if you're not at home or near a bed? Don't worry, there are other ways. A good trick in this situation is to **think of someone worse off than you**. I always think of Peter Hughes, a boy I was at school with in Cardiff. He was an unfortunate-looking fellow with red hair and thick milk bottle style glasses that he was always pushing back up the bridge of his nose, like Ronnie Corbett. Unlike Ronnie, though, people tended to laugh *at* Peter and not with him, which was a shame as he was basically a good boy who was unfortunate enough to be afflicted with both red hair and diabetes. In fact, that's what they used to call him in school, Dai Abetes, Dai being short for David in Welsh and, purely by chance, also Peter's middle name. Peter's school days were a misery as Phil McLennan, one of the McLennan brothers, constantly picked on him; both of the brothers, they weren't big in a physical sense but they were certainly tough, were feared throughout the school. This is often the case: **look at Tom Cruise**. Peter would wince whenever one of them came near. Then one day he just cracked and in a scene reminiscent of Sylvester Stallone in *First Blood* lashed out in anger, stabbing McLennan with his insulin injection! Actually, thinking about it, this incident predates *First Blood* by four or five years, Peter was ahead of his time. All the boys cheered as Phil hit the floor, writhing around in agony, and Peter was hoisted shoulder high, arms aloft, punching the air, again like Sylvester Stallone, this time in *Rocky II*. Suddenly though the mood changed; one of the other boys was checking on Phil and found that he had stopped breathing. Horror filled the air as we realized what had happened. Peter had killed Phil McLennan! As we all rushed to see for ourselves, Peter fell from the shoulders of the boy that was carrying him, Alan Whitby, and in doing so broke his wrist on the hard playground floor. The whole thing went to court and it looked like Peter would be sent to prison, again like Sylvester Stallone, this time in *Lock Up* (1989), but it was found that Peter was too young to be tried for murder and so he walked free. Right or wrong? I'm not going to sit in judgement; but I will say I think it's wrong. There were no winners in the whole affair. Andrew McLennan had to adjust to life without his beloved and violent brother while the Hughes family were forced to move to Neath.

Incidentally, while on the subject of insulin injections it's interesting to note that you are no longer allowed to take injections onto airplanes for fear of them being used as weapons in this terrorist age. **I think this is sensible**; after all it stands to reason that a certain percentage of terrorists *must* be diabetic. By which I don't mean that it's a job requirement! I'm not saying that they turn up for the interview and are told, "I'm sorry, Mr Al Fazad, but your blood sugar levels are perfectly normal, I'm afraid we've got nothing for you at the moment... Try Hezbollah!" Of course I'm not, but equally, what if it's one of the goodies, one of the Americans who's diabetic and goes to use his insulin injection to overpower a terrorist, not realizing that the terrorist himself is also diabetic and in stabbing him inadvertently boosts his strength? You'd be kicking yourself! It's a minefield, an absolute minefield.

One thing shines through the minefield and that is this: There's always someone worse off than you. Always. And if there isn't then you can comfort yourself with the knowledge that someone else is gaining strength and comfort from looking at you and thinking that at least there's someone worse off than them; for after all, without a loser there can be no winners!

My Dad's a (Super) Hero

Finally, when it comes to the little smashers, all parents, and particularly Dads, want to be a hero in the eyes of their child. This is perfectly understandable, but how can we achieve it? Especially if the Dad in question isn't residing at the same domicile (not my words, the words of the court. You can't fight City Hall! Hoo Ha!!) it can be difficult to impress your heroic qualities from the other end of the motorway. Difficult, but not impossible… Here are some easy-to-follow suggestions of ways to appear heroic to your children:

Is it a bird? Is it a plane? No, it's Dad!

1. If you wear glasses, follow the example of Clark Kent aka Superman and take them off when you do something difficult,[1] like lifting a heavy box or helping to push a cow into a cattle truck.

---

1 except when driving

2. When consuming soft drinks in the presence of the children, choose the small "airline" size cans. These make your hands appear larger than they are. When you've finished drinking, smile confidently and crush the can with ease.

3. If you're allowed to attend your child's birthday party, go the whole hog and dress up as a known superhero; this will subliminally reinforce the notion of heroism and is relatively easy to achieve. Most towns have a fancy dress shop; if you can't find one, try the internet. N.B. Be warned: It is important to keep a check on emotions when dressed as Spiderman or Superman. The costumes are hot and tempers can become raised; if this *does* happen, go and sit down somewhere on ground level to cool off. Do not, repeat DO NOT climb any building/tree/crane while dressed as a superhero or you could have another Fathers for Justice debacle on your hands. When it comes to dads dressed as comic book heroes, the police are quite definite in their stance. I must say though that the staff at the station are a lot more pleasant than the arresting officers, who let's face it are under an awful lot of stress.

Role-play

In this role-play we are going to put into practice the techniques we have learnt in this step. That is: how to say something in such a way as to present it in the best possible light. The scenario is as follows: You and your partner have been going through a rocky patch, there has been tension in the air and tempers have been raised. Your partner is a dog lover; nothing gives her more pleasure than Bonnie, your faithful old Border Collie. One day Bonnie slips away peacefully in her sleep. You know only too well how much this will upset your partner; you have to tread carefully.[1] Particularly around Bonnie, a clumsy accident around her would only add insult to injury. What do you tell your partner? Re-read this chapter before you decide; if you read it carefully enough you will find all the clues you need to make the right decision.

OK, here we go.

HER I'm home!

YOU Sit down; I've got something to tell you…

HER What is it?

How do you reply?

A: The dog's dead.

B: You know how we can never get away on holiday because we're always looking after old Bonnie? Well, not any more! She's gone to a better place and now so can we. Let's celebrate! Whoo! Hey! Ya!

---

1 Bonnie isn't really dead, she never existed.

C: We're going to save on dog food.

Choose carefully, good luck!

NOW I KNOW

* A confused dog can eat its own tail.

* George Michael is gay.

* We must communicate clearly.

* Aunty Jean has died.

Decree Nice Guy

*The Marriage is Over…
the Friendship Begins*

"Let's be friends"

BRUCE SPRINGSTEEN – LET'S BE FRIENDS

"You're my best friend"

QUEEN – YOU'RE MY BEST FRIEND

"You've got a friend"

JAMES TAYLOR – YOU'VE GOT A FRIEND

This is such an important, vital step in *Making Divorce Work*, the post-marriage friendship. It's a step that many find difficult; I appreciate that, but have to say that in my own case I have been blessed with, if anything, **a *better* relationship with Marion now than when we were married**. Why? Hard to say, although I think the **distance helps**. We're far less under each other's feet these days and that can keep the freshness alive. With her in Cardiff and me in London, we seem to have found the perfect set-up. The M4 motorway is a lifeline for us both, a vital artery and also an arm, in as much as it keeps us at arm's length. (Her analogy, not mine, but I think it works!)

I never thought that a man could feel affection for a motorway, but I do! For me, the M4 is the yellow brick road. Why? Because, because, because, because, because… it's the road that takes me to my two little smashers and each time I gaily skip down it, my heart lifts. Let me be quite clear, I don't actually skip; I drive. Skipping on a motorway, even on the hard shoulder, would constitute jaywalking and as such would be rightly considered a criminal offence. This book in no way endorses such reckless, anti-social and, most importantly, **dangerous** behaviour. I've done the journey so many times now I know it like the back of my hand and could do it with my eyes shut! In fact I **did** do it with my eyes shut once; **a terrible mistake**, a **complete error of judgement** and **something that I sorely regret**. Luckily no one was harmed. I came to a halt on the hard shoulder unscathed and, better still, undetected by the police. It was four-thirty in the morning and they had better things to do than caution a sleepy dad! And anyway, they didn't have to; the experience was **terrifying** and taught me a valuable lesson. I'm sure that there are many men, and women, although if we're being honest it's predominantly men, who make their own joyous journey up the motorway to visit their own little smashers. It's a modern-day ritual and I'm proud to be a part of it. This contact is vital for the dads and kids alike. Being with the children keeps you centred, keeps your feet on the ground. If I didn't have my three hours with them every four weeks, I'd be away with the fairies. The journey itself can be almost as enjoyable as the time spent with the little ones if you know what to do. I've compiled a list of ways to enhance the trip down the motorway, what I call "**the daddy dash**", and make it even more enjoyable.

Daddy Dash Dos & Don'ts

• DO allow plenty of time for your journey. Although most of Britain's motorways run smoothly, there are sometimes jams that can put your time back by up to twenty minutes.

- DON'T drive drunk. Seems obvious, but look at the figures!

- DO make a note of places of interest along the way, theme parks, castles, factory outlets, farms, cinema multiplexes, etc., that could prove useful once full access has been granted.

- DON'T arrive too early. Your visiting time will be specified. Respect it.

- DO take presents or the cash equivalent.

- DON'T exceed the speed limit.

- DO drive on the left.

As I've said, my own journey is a particularly pleasant one, taking me from the hustle, bustle and grime of London to the green leafy pastures of Cardiff. From the outset, as I approach the elevated section of the M4, **my heart is pounding** as I speculate on my impending meeting. I'm thinking of my little smashers of course. Will they be pleased to see me? Will they have grown? Will they be in? My hopes soar along with the car as we climb high over Brentford and, to a lesser extent, Chiswick. This section of the journey always strikes me as quite

 glamorous, the environment has an almost Los Angeles like quality to it, as you can see from the photograph, taken by myself on a recent trip. You could almost imagine Billy Joel cruising along in an open-top American car.

These mighty skyscrapers wouldn't look out of place in a Spider Man movie! Note the tall building in the centre, headquarters for GlaxoSmithKline, the people that make Lemsip! Although you can't *buy* a Lemsip there, as I found out to my cost! A lovely chap, Leighton, the security guard, three months away from retirement on the day we met. As he said to me, "Keith, you're wasting my time and yours." Fair enough.

Up, Up and Away!

After the Lemsip building and the Heston Services, the next place of note is of course Heathrow Airport, which can be seen from the motorway as you head west. Just crane your neck to the left and there she is! **Britain's busiest airport** and soon to be blessed with a fifth terminal, Heathrow is a wonderful achievement of engineering and vision. I'm not a good flier, I can find the experience tense and anxiety-laden though I do enjoy going to the airport. The ideal scenario for me is to **drop off a friend**. I park up in the Short Stay, help my friend with their bags, *it's not always a friend, sometimes it can be the friend of a friend*, then just soak up **the atmosphere of international travel**. Lovely. Obviously, when I'm bombing down to Cardiff to see the kids I don't actually stop off at the airport; that would be madness, not to mention prohibitively time consuming. No, what I'll do then is just a quick couple of times round the perimeter fence, a friendly wave to the plane-spotters and I'm on my way, *adios amigos*!

A Very Nice Man

After Heathrow it's plain sailing for a while; keen **Royalists are in for a treat** as we pass within view of Windsor Castle, scene of so many Royal events over the years, while **chocolate lovers** will get a king-size kick as we pass Slough, home of the Mars Bar! Next up on the map is Reading, famed of course for Reading Gaol, where Oscar Wilde was incarcerated in May of 1895, but that's not what interests *us* about Reading! Of more note to us Daddy Dashers are the wonderful new motorway services, recently opened, that straddle the M4 like a mighty colossus, providing everything the weary traveller needs: food, drink, petrol, audio books, video games and **instant RAC membership**. I well remember one visit in the autumn of 2003 when I got chatting to the resident RAC salesman, Bob, a super Yeovil man, now in his sixties. He had a lovely gimmick: his name was Robert (Bob) Andrew Collins… RAC! He had a lot of fun with this, asking people if they wanted to join *his* organization, then, when their attention had been gained, he would explain his initials. **I found it fascinating** and could listen to him until the cows came home, in fact on one trip I'd already stocked up on sweets and things at Heston but still called in at Reading **just to hear the story again**; it was that good! A natural performer, **like Jimmy Nail**, Bob could have whole coach parties eating out of his hand as he wove his magic; but be warned! If I've whetted your appetite for a little Bob Collins moment, **he's no longer there**. The last three times it's been a Londoner, what I call a Cockney, called Steve who, while I'm sure he's a lovely man, falls very short of Bob's standards of salesmanship and sheer charisma. I asked what had happened to Bob and Steve said he'd been moved to the Welcome Break at Membury, but I've never seen him there. Bob, if you're reading this, then… Obviously if you are reading this it would suggest that **things haven't worked out with you and Joyce.** That's a real shame, my friend. I never had the pleasure of meeting your good lady, but just from those few photos you showed me I think I got a feel of her. I can honestly say that I've never been more impressed by someone I didn't meet than by your Joyce, she was a jewel. But hey ho, onwards and upwards! As this book shows, there is life after divorce, and it's for living! It won't be long before you **find a new lady** ready to join the RAC, and it won't be roadside assistance she's looking for! No, to quote your own lovely joke on the subject, it'll be *bedside* assistance!

Anyway, we can't linger on the breakdown of Bob's marriage; we've got to hit the road. Just around the Reading Services area there's a man-made lake where people go jet skiing; it looks

smashing but unless you're stuck in traffic it's unlikely that you'll get a decent look at it. If you are lucky enough to encounter a jam in this area, it's to the left as you head westbound.

Some lovely scenery now as we make our way towards Wales. There *are* two more service options open to us, Membury and Leigh Delamere. In their day both were fine examples of the genre, able to hold their heads up high; but now in this new-millennium, post-Reading age they seem sadly inadequate and, unless Nature's Call is pressing too strongly, I recommend that you give them both a miss.

Bridge Over Troubled Water

And so we come to what for me represents the pinnacle of the journey, a chance to stand and gawp in awe at man's ability to **harness** the elements and overcome all natural obstacles. The New Severn Crossing, aka The Severn Bridge. If you've never been then I urge you, go! It's a real treat and you only pay one way. Leaving Wales is free of charge but it will

cost you £4.60 to get in; that's OK, pay once at the entrance then all the rides are free! It's a bit of fun. Seriously though, just look at it, isn't it beautiful?

A triumph of science and nature, it's been a favourite of mine since its opening on the 5th of June 1996 (I was there!) and is more than just a cable-stayed construction bridge. It's a wonderful spot for quiet contemplation and its staff are friendly beyond belief. I recently parked up on the English side one evening and strolled out to the mid-point of the bridge from where the view is breathtaking! Above me, sky and the sound of sea birds, below me the deep and dark abyss. I'd only been out there for ten minutes when one of the stewards came and joined me. Above all else it was his level of **courtesy and politeness** that impressed me most; wary that I was savouring a private moment of quiet contemplation he approached me ever so quietly, so as not to disturb me. Then, when he was about ten feet away, gently held out his hand and asked my name. This level of friendliness is quite out of the ordinary nowadays and I was momentarily lost for words. "That's all right," he said, "You don't need to talk if you don't want to…" Lovely. I don't think his head for heights was quite as steady as mine though; he was soon asking me to step away from the edge, which I did. I didn't want to make him nervous. Anyway, we strolled over the bridge together and called in at his office for a cup of tea and a biscuit, where he was much more chatty. Quite the talk show host. It was like having a cup of tea with Jonathon Ross or Patrick Kielty!

He wanted to know everything about me! How I was feeling in myself, how was work, **who was my next of kin?** We chatted for up to an hour, I even met some of his colleagues, who I'm sure had better things to do than sit and chat to me as I filled in form after form…

Before we move on from the bridge, it is worth noting that it's not all fun, games and laughter. There is a dark side to the bridge, which it would be wrong to shy away from: **many have tried to take their own lives here**. Most recently of course there was that terrible episode when the former drummer of The Stereophonics went missing; very sad, he certainly didn't "Have A Nice Day" and the band haven't been the same since.

The Land of My Fathers

Obviously, once you're over the bridge, it's official; you're in Wales! Welcome! Welcome to Wales! **It's a lovely place** and the people will waste no time in making you feel welcome; they're too busy! Not really, I would never say that, it's a bit of fun. Seriously though, this part of the journey is something of a blur to me as I'm roughly half an hour away from arriving at my destination. I'll make a quick stop at the Magor Services, to clear the car of cans and crisp packets and chocolate wrappers. I'll stand up and **brush down my lap**, then plug in my car vac for a quick once over the front section of the car. The back seats are fine, they remain untouched for the duration of the journey, but the front can look like a bomb has hit it. Admittedly a very friendly chocolate and crisp bomb, but still quite a mess none the less. I'll also fill up with petrol at this point as it means that I then have **a full tank for the remainder of the outward journey** as well as just about enough for the return leg. It's not too far a distance, one hundred and fifty-six miles door to door, or three hundred and twelve there and back. Or, as once happened when I realized I'd left something behind just as I got back, six hundred and twenty-four. That was the journey I mentioned earlier where I ended up on the hard shoulder!

So, with the car looking like a new pin and with a full tank of petrol, you're ready to set off once again.[1] There's not much else of interest on the journey. Between Newport and Cardiff look out on the right for the Celtic Manor Resort, a huge hotel with spa facilities and an enormous golf course which has attracted many top golfers from around the world, including Ronnie Corbett.

---

1 The petrol forecourt at Magor is on a slight slope. On one occasion I got out of the car a bit too quickly; this combined with a degree of light-headedness and nerves at the prospect of seeing my little smashers, plus a fairly oily forecourt, meant that I lost my footing. I stumbled sideways between the car and the pump and caught a glancing blow to the head as I fell. To this day I can't be sure whether it was the car or the pump with which I collided. It doesn't matter; I was out cold. I came to in a matter of minutes but the damage was done; my confidence was dented, loose change was lost and I had an oily print all down my right side which meant that on my arrival Marion refused me entry to the house.

Hands Across the Water

And so I arrive! Thanks to a simple stretch of road that has proved **a lifeline in my divorce**. The house itself, on the outskirts of Cardiff, is not the same one in which Marion and I shared so many happy times; it's considerably bigger. It's a lovely red brick detached building in a beautiful gated private estate. Like the one O.J. Simpson lived in. It has its own driveway, which can take **up to six cars** although I always park on the road so that Geoff's *Humvee*, his big American four-wheel-drive vehicle, can come and go with ease. I think they prefer it this way; in fact I *know* they prefer it. Actually that's my abiding image of Geoff, sat behind the wheel of his big black High Mobility Multipurpose Wheeled Vehicle and grinning like Jack Nicholson as he steers *The Beast*, as he calls it, towards me as I make my way carefully up the drive. To be fair to him, he always steers the other way at the last minute! That's Geoff; he's in control. I can't say enough about Geoff. When a divorce hits you, whether you're a man or a woman, but particularly when you're a man, the great worry is, "Who will the new partner be?" Well in Geoff **Marion hit the jackpot**. In a funny way so did I. It's what I call a **win-win** situation!

I'm truly blessed with her choice of man; in Geoff she's found a real Prince who has stepped in and taken over the tiller, as it were, of my marriage with the consummate ease that befits a team leader of one of this country's leading pharmaceutical companies. **The ship is in good hands!** This aspect of divorce, what I call *getting to know your ex-partner's new* *partner*, is once again a vital one. Let's not get caught up in it here, though, as I deal with it extensively in Step 7, Old Friends, New Friends: Getting to Know Your Ex-Partner's New Partner.

For now we are more concerned with the relationship between you and your ex; how to nurture it, tend to it and watch it grow in that difficult period after the divorce. If there are children involved then of course you are going to have to maintain a healthy relationship with their mother, only **a fool** would say otherwise. Sometimes though, when there are no children on the scene, **experts advise the divorcing parties to have nothing to do with each other** once the finances are settled. This is the general opinion, **endorsed the world over by leading authorities** and **marriage specialists**. While I'm not saying **they're wrong**, I would never say that, I don't think they're necessarily right either.

Keep in Touch

Simple advice, but vital! Don't let the divorce stop you from staying in touch with someone you once loved enough to marry! You've got so much in common with them, as you have with their new partner, although again that is covered in more detail in Step 7, Old Friends, New Friends: Getting to Know Your Ex-Partner's New Partner. You've already lost the marriage; to lose touch as well would be awful. For all you know, you could end up getting back together! I appreciate that if you're reading this soon after the break-up then *getting back together* might seem the last thing you'd want to do. I know that some people have very **bitter break-ups** and come away harbouring all sorts of **unpleasant thoughts** about their exes, but even so, KEEP IN TOUCH. You don't have to look far to find examples of couples that **couldn't stand each other** to such an extent that they divorced, only to then go and **remarry each other** soon after…

DO IT AGAIN!

• Melanie Griffith and Don Johnson.

• Elizabeth Taylor and Richard Burton.

• Natalie Wood and Robert Wagner.

Fair enough, that's not a very lengthy list; in all honesty **I was expecting it to be much longer**. But I think my point still stands. Consider this, if Nicolas Cage and Lisa Marie Presley, Bruce Willis and Demi Moore and Nicole Kidman and Tom Cruise were to remarry, the list would double. Also, this is just a list of **celebrities** that are known to have remarried each other. In the **real world** it is harder to tell as no records are kept, but surely it must happen. I knew a boy at school who went on to get married to Nicola Pearson. They divorced after four years and he is now married to her sister Fran. It's not the same as marrying the same person again but it's close.

The Impossible Dream

As you've been reading this step, what thoughts have been running through your mind? Have they been along the following lines?

"Hmm, yes, this is all making sense…"

"Keith seems to be hitting the nail on the head."

"Gosh, this is exactly how I view the world. How refreshing to encounter a kindred spirit. It's like finding a long-lost twin."

Or are you perhaps the sort of person who would react in this way?

"For Pete's sake, what the heck is the fool talking about now? I've just about had enough!"

Let us for the sake of argument say that your reaction was closer to that last response than to the former. This is a shame, a great shame. We now live in an age when people shy away from challenges and I can't help thinking that if some of the great British achievers of the past were to suddenly spring back to life, they would be hugely disappointed by what they saw. Isambard Kingdom Brunel, Charles Darwin, Oliver Cromwell, William Shakespeare would all be turning in their graves at the way modern men are prepared to drift away from their wives after a divorce. Even Winston Churchill, winner of the BBC's excellent series *Great Britons*, would say something like, "Are my eyes deceiving me?"

For the fact of the matter is that there's no reason for you not to stay on good terms with your ex and go on to do what the title of this step suggests, "*Letting the Friendship Begin*". How can this be achieved? Let's turn once again to our friend Paul McKenna. In his best-selling book, *The Number One Bestseller Change Your Life In Seven Days, Includes Free Mind Programming CD*, Paul talks at some length about a technique that has served him well over the years, **visualization**.

VISUALIZATION

It's a big word, but what exactly does it mean? Our old friend the dictionary tells us that it is *a technique used to produce an image of an internal organ or other part of the body by using X-rays or other means such as magnetic resonance imaging*, but this is almost certainly not what Paul is talking about. This is a medical interpretation of the word and is of no use to us here; indeed if you have recently lost a loved one to a disease affecting internal organs then this brief passage will have caused you untold upset and tears, dredging up painful episodes from your recent past. For this I apologize. No, the interpretation we need is the one before; this is what Paul McKenna is talking about: *a technique whereby somebody creates a vivid positive mental picture of something such as a desired outcome to a problem, in order to promote a sense of well-being*. Bingo! It is interesting to note that although my first interpretation didn't work out, I didn't sink into a pit of despair and refuse to try again. Think of the first interpretation as a first wife; do you see my point? Exactly!

Paul is talking about visualizing that which we want. In his book he gives a **wonderful example** of something that happened to him a while ago. Over to you, Paul:

"One time, I went into a Mercedes showroom and sat in a car to get comfortable. I smelled the leather, went for a test drive and imagined it was my own. I took away a brochure to add to my scrapbook and imagined driving it every day. Pretty soon, my mind was focused upon getting me one and I began to see Mercedes everywhere. Before long, a seeming coincidence brought a bargain deal my way, and I bought my first Mercedes."

Inspirational stuff, like *Rocky*, but would it work for the ordinary man or woman in the street, or is it only effective in the **hands of a mystic?** I put Paul's technique to the test and visited a local Mercedes showroom. Like Paul I sat in the car. Like Paul I smelled the leather. This is where things started to go wrong. With hindsight I can see that when he talks about "smelling the leather" he probably means a quick subtle whiff; in other words, *acceptable smelling*. I can now see that my **excessive smelling** at close range to the beautiful leather upholstery was inappropriate, unnecessary and worrying to the showroom staff. All credit to them, though; I was asked to vacate the premises in a firm but friendly voice and no harm was done to my person. I bear you no ill!

Undeterred, I visited another showroom, this time keeping the smelling down to an acceptable minimum. A test drive was granted with Howard the salesman, a lovely chap who kept me entertained with stories of his son who works in the media, and I left the showroom with a brochure and a free key ring. So far, so good! All I need now is a *seeming coincidence* and the car will be mine.

The scrapbook that Paul mentions is just that – a collection of pictures or articles relating to your dreams. Things that you can look at and visualize achieving while you wait for the *seeming coincidence*. This is a wonderful technique to employ when trying to engineer a reunion with your ex-spouse.

A Photograph of You

"A photograph of you"
A FLOCK OF SEAGULLS – PHOTOGRAPH OF YOU

"Who got the camera?"
ICE CUBE – WHO GOT THE CAMERA

"My camera never lies"
BUCKS FIZZ – MY CAMERA NEVER LIES

We all had scrapbooks as children, cutting and pasting in bits and bobs on our heroes and heroines. If we think back I'm sure we can all remember the **fun** they gave us. Well, they can be just as much fun as a grown up. If you really want to get back with your ex then let's take a leaf out of Paul McKenna's book and start compiling scrapbooks so that we can visualize being back together with the one we love.

The scrapbook itself is easy to come by; all high street stationers stock a good range at reasonable prices; once purchased your next requirement is glue. If you've not bought glue for a while, let me tell you that things have moved on! It's no longer pots and brushes like they used to have on *Blue Peter*, nowadays the king of the hill is Pritt, a handy little glue in a tube, again available at most high street stationers. Now comes the hard bit! What to put in…

The important thing and really the purpose of the scrapbook is to keep in touch or at least *feel* as though you are keeping in touch with your ex, through visualization. **Photographs are one of the best ways to visualize**, so the first thing to do is to gather together however many photos you still have from happier times together.

- The Engagement Party

- The Wedding

- The Honeymoon

- The Birth of Your First Child

- The Birth of Your Second Child, etc.

- Holidays

- Wedding Anniversaries

Let's hope that you still have as many of these sort of photographs as possible. I know that lots of people throw them away when they split up, and that's a real shame. Once these photos are selected and displayed you are ready to move on to the most exciting and challenging part of the process.

FRESH PICKINGS

This is when you can start to become creative and use your imagination, as you become private detective and paparazzi photographer all in one, because it's vital that you begin to generate NEW photographs if your visualization is to work. By only using **old** photographs you will simply visualize the past. What I call

remembering

and while this can be enjoyable, it is no substitute for true visualization. So get to work straight away, take your camera and get snapping! What sort of photographs? All sorts. At home, at work, at play... Hanging out the washing, dropping the kids off at school, in the park with the new husband, that sort of thing. Basically you are trying to build up a solid picture of the kind of life you would like to be having with her yourself. Remember not to get too close, this kind of project is essentially a covert operation and secrecy is paramount. Once you've gathered a sufficient amount of photos, it's time to turn detective. If your ex has remarried, you have a great opportunity for visualization through her new wedding photos. Obviously I'm not saying you should creep into her house while she's out and steal them! That would be madness and also a criminal offence. What I'm suggesting is meticulous research at your local newspaper offices, combing through their collection of wedding day pictures. Once located, cut off the husband's head and insert your own; this will speed the visualization process considerably. Better still, if you are a computer whiz, you can interfere with the photos digitally.

The bottom line is this: there's very little that you can't achieve through visualization. If your dream is to be back with your wife and children then simply…

Dream On

NOW I KNOW

* The friendship needn't die
  when the love does.

* Visualization works.

* The M4 holds many hidden treasures.

* Remarrying your ex is not impossible.

* There's a really great view
  from the Severn Bridge.

Step

7

Old Friends, New Friends

*Getting to Know Your
Ex-Partner's New Partner*

"Johnny come lately, the new kid in town..."

THE EAGLES – THE NEW KID IN TOWN

"Like to get to know you well"

HOWARD JONES – LIKE TO GET TO KNOW YOU WELL

"You're my best friend"

QUEEN – YOU'RE MY BEST FRIEND

This is a thorny area. For some people the mere thought of their ex being with someone else is **like a red rag to a bull**, they see red, the steam starts to pour out of their ears and we all have to run for cover. It can be like watching a scene from *The Incredible Hulk*; not the original and rather tame TV series with Bill Bixby but the recent film adaptation with the man from Brad Pitt's reinterpretation of *Troy* in it. Men can get tamping mad at the thought of their ex with a new man and will sometimes let their feelings get the better of them with a dreadful display of foul-mouthed yelling. Often it will go further than that and escalate into all-out, full-on man-to-man violence with both parties coming away battered and bruised; with the lady in question left crying and shaking on the sidelines, yelling, "No, Geoff, leave it! Please leave it! He's not worth it."

Why?

I think it's a sense of self-protection, a fear that any new lover will be privy to **all your secrets**. The horrible thought that your ex-wife will tell the new man intimate details of private moments, pointing out your shortcomings with glee. Sharing **private moments** that you had considered precious and sacred. That walk along the river when you proposed to her, the weekend in Cornwall when it rained so much you couldn't leave the room or, God forbid, the holiday in Cyprus when you met Dave and Carla from Leeds, you all had too much to drink and events took an unexpected turn. You'd never do something like that again and it was completely out of character; more to do with the heat than anything else... The fear that he will then spread this new-found knowledge amongst his friends at the squash club and they in turn will hand it to **Peter Lewis in I.T.** and he will post the tape on the internet. Setting up a **pay-per-view** site similar to the terrible ones dedicated to Pamela Anderson and Tommy Lee and Paris Hilton and her boyfriend. The ensuing notoriety leads to you **losing your job**. Your friends and family soon follow suit and you're left **homeless and penniless** until as a last resort you commit a **random act of violence**, what I call *going postal*, in a public place. You are then sentenced to a brief spell in prison; while inside you become addicted to drugs. On your release you roam the streets with nothing but a dog for friendship, finding shelter where you can on a night-to-night basis.

These are all rational fears, but trust me; they needn't come to pass.

Your ex-partner's new partner *needn't* be an enemy, **he can be a friend**, he can be a **partner for you as well as your wife** (in the sense that Starsky is Hutch's partner) if only for the sake of the children, even if there *are* no children. This is a person, man or woman, it doesn't matter which; probably a man, about six foot, dark hair, glasses when he drives; who rightly or wrongly has attracted the person with whom…

a. You were once **in love**.

b. You thought was the **perfect match**.

c. With whom you once saw your future. Maybe you still do, in which case this is going to be a painful chapter… Although who's to say that you won't get back together? *They* **say it, obviously**. But they would, wouldn't they? What do they know? They don't understand her like you do. To an extent their families say it, to a lesser extent your family says it and of course the children chip in now and again. But that doesn't mean they're right. After all, you can lead a horse to water… Whatever you do, don't rule it out just because others say it's impossible. Thirty years ago they said man would never colonize Saturn.

The point is this: already, even before meeting him, you know that you have similar tastes, you are attracted to the same things, you both saw the **beauty** in the woman he now calls his.

You've Got Something in Common!

"Commonality" is **the cornerstone foundation of any friendship**. Who knows? You could have loads more in common, many shared interests and opinions that could draw you together to bond, but you won't know until you become proper friends. But be careful! Like any courtship you'll need to **tread gently towards your target**, gathering information about him along the way, before finally approaching with the fully extended hand of friendship; thus retaining the element of surprise!

How do you do this? It sounds a little daunting, quite a challenge you might say. Well, relax; there's never been a better time to gather background information on a suspect. In the old days you'd have been stuck with making discreet enquiries amongst mutual friends, wandering the streets with a fading photograph, asking questions in his local pub and **sitting outside his flat in your car**. Nowadays everything is different. You can find out reams of information, **highly personal information**

about a person from the comfort of your own home and all you need is a computer. That's right, the internet!

We're all familiar with search engines like Google, but did you know that there are services that are specifically tailored to finding out more about a person? So, fingers on mice, and off we go…

- **192.com**. A wonderful service that can help you to build up a more rounded picture of the new man in her life.

- **Peoplesite.com**. Predominantly for runaways but don't rule it out.

- **Omnitrace.com**

- **1stlocate.co.uk**. No success, no fee!

- **Iklocate.com**. Names, addresses, births, deaths and marriages.

- **familyfinding.co.uk**. Get the lowdown on his family.

- **Peoplespot.com**. They can help you find his phone number.

- **Web-detective.com**. Public and criminal records, F.B.I. anything about anyone!

You will also need a modem, ideally broadband. At time of going to press BT Broadband Basic have an offer of £19.99 a month with free installation. Call 0800 800 060. In the interests of fairness, Telewest Blueyonder also offer a service from £17.99 a month with installation currently free (for a limited period). I can't be seen to influence your decision but I will say that the BT one looks good.

- **Where's Wally?** Not a website but an amusing book-based game that can take your mind off things and help you to see the funny side of your awful situation. It's a bit of fun!

Piecing it Together

**"I'm offering you a psychological profile
of Buffalo Bill..."**

ANTHONY HOPKINS – THE SILENCE OF THE LAMBS.

Just like the early days of a new friendship at primary school, getting to know your ex-partner's new partner is a **wonderful, exciting process**, so why not break the ice with a game of conkers? Not really, that would be ridiculous, but finding a common ground, an interest that you both share, other than your ex-wife, is an excellent idea when you're searching for ways to cement the friendship in its early stages. Right from the outset there are some very basic questions that need answering:

- **What does he like to do?**

- **Who does he like to do it with?**

- **Would he like to do it with you?**

This information can be harvested from the smallest seed of knowledge. All you need to know is **where he went to school**; with that little nugget, it's straight back on the internet and a log in with our chums at Friends Reunited.

Zoom straight in on his school; calculate the year (You'll need to know his age. Think back to the lively conversation with your then wife; "Is it because he's younger than me?" "He's not younger than you, he's … *insert age*) and then register. Choose a non descript, plausible name like Paul, John or Mark… In fact any of the disciples will do. (Steer clear of Judas) Now start to make postings on the message board, but be careful, **don't just jump in head first**, do a little research. Read up on the teachers so that you can appear knowledgeable; you don't want your comment on Mr Johnson, Geography to not ring true. Read up on him, find out that he wore horn-rimmed glasses and then join in the general banter with postings like,

> *What about old Johnson?*
> *He used to wear glasses.*

By doing this you will slip into the cyber school community unnoticed and with no suspicions raised. Then, and only then, you can start to investigate your victim. That's not the right word for it; *suspect*. That's no good either; *quarry*. Equally bad. OK, *your wife's new boyfriend*. There again I'm wide of the mark; she's your *ex* wife's new boyfriend. It's very difficult, and I'm not even personally involved; heaven only knows how it is for you. It's such an emotive subject, you could write a book on it.

Helping with Enquiries

Now that you are in under the wire as it were, it's time to get down to some serious detecting. The full *Miss Marple*! First of all, there is lots of knowledge to be gained without asking a single question. **Simply by listening**, or in this case reading. Read all the things that are said about your man by the other ex-pupils, try and build up a picture. Speaking of pictures, click on the picture section and see if you can spot him in an old school photo. He'll have changed a lot since then but that doesn't matter; we're trying to build up a fully rounded portrait of the man. If you spot him, print off the photo, **blow it up** and put it on the wall of a room at home, for consultation at a later date. Slowly your home can begin to take on the appearance of an incident room from *Cracker* or *Taggart*! Soon you'll want some more recent shots to add to your ever-growing gallery, and for that there's no substitute for a method mentioned a little earlier in this chapter, *sitting outside their house in your car*. Sometimes the old ones are the best! This is a technique that has been employed in detection for years and years; we all remember Paul Michael Glaser and David Soul, sat in their big red Ford Gran Torino, outside the home of a suspected drug baron or small-time crook. In this sense the whole thing can be a bit of fun as you imagine yourself as an LA cop on a heist! If you fancy this course of action, here are some tips to help you along.

STAKEOUT!

- Bring a book.
- Take a camera along with you. Something with a long lens will make you feel the part, but nowadays you can get good prints from a range of reasonably priced cameras, many of them digital. The advantage with digital is that you can **see the picture straight away** and decide whether you got a good shot at his face and want to keep it or not. You also get instant prints with the old Polaroid One, the camera where the picture slides out the front as soon as you've taken it! Be warned though, this is a very noisy camera and you are on **covert operations**. Also, it doesn't have a zoom, so for the sort of thing we're planning it's not suitable. If you've gone ahead and bought a Polaroid already, not to worry; it'll be perfect for when you've got to know your subject a little better and want some instant snaps at parties, nights out, etc…
- Carry a map or A–Z. That way, if someone asks why you've been sat there for the last eight hours you can say that you're looking for Elm Bank Gardens.
- For that real LA stakeout feel, place some fast-food containers on the dashboard.
- Re: above, take a Dictaphone and record yourself saying the sort of things that American police might say, like "All units, all units!" or "Zebra Three, Zebra Three!" If you have the confidence, try it in an American accent… Play the recording back to yourself when things are slow.
- Bring another book.

It's important to remember that all the stages I've described so far in *getting to know your ex-partner's new partner* take place **before you've even met the man**. You may have had a brief meeting, depending on the overall timescale of the breakdown of your marriage, while picking up some belongings or children at the house. For our purposes, though, we will **assume or pretend** that you haven't properly met. The slate is clean. That way we come to the situation without history, what young people call *baggage*. Of course in some situations you may know the man in question all too well. "What do you mean by that, Keith?" I'm talking about when your wife leaves you for **someone that you already know**, someone with whom you already have a relationship. A friend, a family member or in some cases, what I consider the worst of all, the cruellest blow, *your best man!*

Imagine that, losing your wife to your best man! Appalling. It sounds like a plot from *Emmerdale* but it does happen in the real world and actually it needn't be all that bad. This is a letter I received from Alan Thompson, a thirty-nine-year-old hospital porter from Nottingham. He got married to Lisa, his girlfriend of six years, in a super ceremony in Dublin, Lisa's hometown. Three weeks later he was **devastated** to discover that Lisa had been seeing Patrick, the best man. To make matters worse, the relationship had only begun on the wedding night after Alan passed out due to mixing alcohol and **a strong course of antibiotics**. He's now in pieces and doesn't know what to do. Over to Alan…

Dear Keith,

Hello, my name is Alan Thompson; I'm a thirty nine year old hospital porter from Nottingham. I recently married my girlfriend Lisa, whom I'd been seeing for six years in a super ceremony in Dublin, her hometown. Three weeks later I was devastated to discover that she had been seeing my best man Robert and that the affair had begun on my wedding night after I passed out when I mixed alcohol and the antibiotics I was on. I'm in pieces and don't know what to do; can you please help me?

Regards

Alan Thompson.

What **a heartbreaking letter** from Alan. I feel for him and I'm sure you do too. But in a way he's lucky! He's already on such good terms with his *ex-partner's new partner* that he chose to make him his best man. **So much of the work has been done** as he now moves into this new phase of his life.

The friendship with Robert is there, it's solid. All that needs to happen now is to do what psychologists call *reframing*, seeing the situation in a new, better light. Our old friend Paul McKenna is a keen advocate of this technique; in his fantastic book *Change Your Life in Seven Days*, as early as day three he is shouting from the rooftops that:

"Your experience of life is primarily affected by the perspective you view it from. Depending upon the meaning we give to situations or events, we will feel and behave differently."

Powerful stuff, and just the lifeline that Alan is looking for as he bobs about in the sea of heartbreak; **trying to make his pyjama bottoms into a buoyancy aid**. As Paul says, and as I hinted at just a moment ago, all Alan needs to do is to look on his situation in a new way, a different way, a better way, if needs be **a false way**, *it doesn't matter*, so long as it makes him **feel better**. "But Keith, poor Alan must be devastated, what possible positives can he take from this disastrous situation?" OK, I'll tell you. By the way, you say disastrous, I say *interesting*. There are many positives up for grabs. These are just a few that I've come up with off the top of my head; it's an impressive list, especially when you consider that in this area of knowledge **I don't really know what I'm talking about**.

> **"Reasons to be cheerful, one, two, three..."**
>
> IAN DURY AND THE BLOCKHEADS

Admiring the View
OR
How can I see this in a better light?

- You've been **selfless**. Putting your friend first. **Well done**.

- You've been cupid and **shot your arrow** with aplomb.

- Your brief marriage has left you **free** to play the field.

- You'd never have visited Dublin if you hadn't got married.

- If you're now **off the antibiotics**, you've got your health.

- You're free to concentrate on your work at the hospital.
  Great news for the sick, elderly and **infirm**.

- Many people as they get married, at the actual moment of
  saying "I do", experience a **worrying stab** of doubt.
  Maybe *you* did; in which case, "Phew!"

Suddenly, through the use of reframing and putting a good
light on things, we begin to see Alan's situation quite differently and I'm left wondering whether I'm not the only one
who actually rather *envies* the **plucky** Nottingham lad and
wishes I could swap places with him. Not a *Wife Swap*, but a
Life Swap. There we are, TV companies, how about that for an
idea? It's a zinger! You could get Lawrence Llewellyn Bowen
to present it, or if he's not available, Nick Knowles and Lowri
Turner, two pros who as far I can tell are yet to put their
names to a shoddy, inferior television programme.

I must stress though that this scenario, your wife running off with your Best Man, is **a most uncommon one** and is **unlikely to happen to you**. None the less, it's worth considering, if you're about to tie the knot, perhaps asking one of your less physically prepossessing friends to fill the role. Just to be on the safe side!

Filling in the Blanks

So let's not worry about BMB, Best Man Betrayal, let's get back to building up our psychological profile of the new man in our life. So far we've:

- Researched his schooldays.
- Begun the compilation of a dossier.
- Hung around outside his house and taken photos.
- Built up the beginnings of a gallery of shots.

This is good; it gives us an idea of our subject before we **move in for the kill**. Please note that *move in for the kill* is simply an expression, I would never advocate murder, what the Americans call *homicide*, other than in the most extreme conditions and even then only in self-defence. I'm sorry if that disappoints you, if you're a bit of a Gung-Ho all guns blazing type, but there it is. I am essentially a peace-loving man at heart and **will not sanction murder**.

No, when I say *move in for the kill* I'm actually describing something very **lovely** which will be of great benefit both to you and to your ex-partner's new partner; forming the friendship. But how do you start? How do you fire the opening salvo?

Your Move!

Yes! That's the **beautiful thing** about building a friendship with the new man; YOU can start it, YOU can set the pace, the ball is in YOUR court. After your exhaustive research and preparation, you are in the perfect position to decide how to proceed. There are many ways; whenever I'm asked which one I recommend I usually say that it's **a personal choice for the individual involved**, but really speaking I think I only say that to make the person feel important because at the end of the day, in my opinion, you can't beat **a letter**. If you can afford to send it recorded delivery then all the better; you'll have bought yourself some **peace of mind** in as much as you can be sure that it will get where it's going. "But Keith, a letter seems so impersonal when what you're doing is essentially extending the hand of friendship." Yes, I understand your point of view but what *you* have to understand is that I'm not talking about a brief typed note; I'm talking about *a letter*. A proper, handwritten, **ten to twelve page letter** in which you can really express your feelings and if necessary do a few drawings as well. This way he will know that you are an honest man, a sensitive man, an open book. On the subject of books, **don't make the mistake** that so many men make at this delicate stage; don't write a book for him! As touching and genuine a gesture as that might seem to you, there's an above average chance that such an act would only serve to alarm him; **it would be too much**, he'd think you were mad! What I call *a nutter…*

Of course, we're not all Jeffrey Archer; we don't all have the ability to weave magic with words. For many of us the thought of writing a letter can be a very intimidating one, one that fills us with dread. Don't worry, I've taken the time to come up with a helping hand for you. I've prepared a cover-all-eventualities, one-stop-shop letter for you to use; simply copy it onto some nice writing paper and insert the appropriate names in the appropriate places. Good luck!

Dear **his name**,

Congratulations! Your name has been chosen from thousands entered into our prize draw and I'm delighted to tell you that you have won a **this is where those hours sitting outside his flat really pay off. Insert something you know he likes, new car, jet-ski, juice extractor…** *To claim your prize, simply call this number…* **your number, preferably your mobile so you won't be out when he calls** *and speak to one of our operators.*

Not really, I'm only joking! But I would like you to call that number… Allow me to introduce myself. I was once lucky enough to step out with your girlfriend, the lovely **her name** *in fact, we were married. That's right, it's me* **your name***. Maybe she's mentioned me. Maybe she hasn't; it doesn't matter. I'm just writing to wish you all the best and to offer the hand of friendship at this difficult time. The early days of a relationship are often tricky aren't they? Both for you and her, and of course for you and me! Having said that, you've known her name for longer than you've known me; in fact I recently discovered you've known her for even longer than I thought you'd known her, if you get my drift... You little tinker! Still, let's let bygones be bygones, it's all water under the bridge now. I know you'll believe me when I say that I couldn't be happier for you.*

Which is not to say that you haven't got your work cut out! All credit to you for taking on the responsibility of my two little smashers **insert names of your children as and if applicable***, they're wonderful kids as I'm sure you'll discover.*

If there are no kids but there is a pet, now is a good time to bring it up, to give a sense of passing on the baton in the big relay race of life, be it in the form of a cat, a dog or a hamster.

Keep an eye on **insert pet's name***, he/she tends to moult and will need worming in June, so think on. He/she was this man's best friend; I hope they'll soon become yours. Anyway, I haven't* written to you just so we could chat about worming tablets! It's really so that we can introduce ourselves and arrange to meet up; at your convenience of course.

I notice that you play squash on Tuesday evenings before popping in to see your Mum. If the last six Tuesdays are anything to go by, you tend to have a window of fifteen to twenty minutes in between these two activities. How about then? I could pop down the squash club and we could have a drink. I think this is a super idea, a neutral location, a place for men to meet! Anyway, don't rush into a decision; I know how busy you are; no, I really do! Karate on Monday at eight, squash and Mum Tuesday, Rugby Thursday at 7.30, your time is not your own sir, your time is not your own. I don't know how you do it! But I do know where...

Well, that's all for now, I look forward to your call. Give my love to **her name and their names if applicable.**

All the best,

Your name

P.S. I've enclosed some drawings.

There we are, **it's a winner!** An excellent way of breaking the ice, laying down the gauntlet and opening the batting, all in one go. Put on your imaginary glasses and imagine the new man sitting down at his desk, taking out his letter opener and reading your words. Picture this in your mind, see him as clearly as you can see your own feet. What is he wearing? Now **listen to him**, hear him breathe, in out, in out, maybe a slight cough. Is he an asthmatic? It's unlikely but, if he is, pop in a gentle wheeze. **Build up this mental film layer by layer, piece by piece until you can see how he reacts to what he finds in your letter**.

In your mind, how is he reacting? Puzzlement? Maybe. Anger? No, definitely not. Pleasure? Is he smiling? Yes he is! It's a hit; **your letter is a big hit!** Look, he's dancing round the room waving the letter in the air; now he's skipping through to the kitchen where your ex-wife is cooking with the children. They're **hugging each other with glee** as they reread your words. What a wonderful mental image you've created. Well done!

> *"When you do get an actual response from him, hang on to this mental image, hold it close to you, like a shield."*

Kick Off!

Well, there we are; do you remember how I earlier likened getting to know your ex-partner's new partner to **the first day at primary school**? Well, we return to that analogy now as, just like a concerned parent, I have to let go of your hand and back away slowly but firmly as you stand there before me **crying and shaking uncontrollably**. It's upsetting for me, it's upsetting for you, there's no getting away from it, that's just how it is. But with all that you've learned from this step, I've every confidence that you'll soon be looking on her man as a new player in **your very own team**; of which you are the captain. Sometimes, when your ex finds herself with a very successful, dynamic man, what I call an Alpha Male, it can feel like *he* is the captain and you are just one of the team. Sometimes just **a substitute**, sat on the bench with **no hope** of getting your tracksuit off! That's OK.

> *Before you let him into your life you were*
> *a lone sprinter…*
> *Now you are part of the team!*

> *Or squad.*

Role-play

In this role-play I want you to imagine yourself in the shoes of your ex-partner's new partner…   Don't worry, it's nothing kinky! It's a process of visualization that will help you understand how he is feeling and at the same time help *you* to feel better about *yourself*.

The scenario is as follows: Your ex-partner and her new partner are in the loft at your old home, looking at some old photos they found in a box while having a clear-out in preparation for a loft conversion to be undertaken while they are away for the summer at the new partner's family's holiday home in Ireland. Amongst the photographs are some old ones of you…

YOUR EX-PARTNER Oh, God, look who it is…

YOUR EX-PARTNER'S NEW PARTNER Is that *insert name*?

YOUR EX-PARTNER Yes it is.

YOUR EX-PARTNER'S NEW PARTNER Wow, he looks great!

That's it! It's as simple as that. A wonderful, positive and uplifting role-play that will make you feel good about yourself and good about the new man. Don't worry if you feel no effect after the first reading, the secret to this one is repetition, also being able to properly visualize your ex-partner's new partner's face as you recite (see STAKEOUT! earlier in this step). Good luck!

NOW I KNOW

* Some people can't bear the thought of beginning
a relationship with their ex-partner's new partner.

* Holiday friendships can turn sour.

* Everyone loves a letter.

* The price of broadband has come down dramatically.

8

Land Ahoy!

Setting Sail for Happiness…

"I am sailing"

    ROD STEWART – SAILING

"Sail on, silver girl, sail on by"

    SIMON AND GARFUNKEL – BRIDGE OVER TROUBLED WATER

"I will go sailing no more"

    MICHAEL CRAWFORD – THE DISNEY ALBUM

Well here we are, we've reached Step 8 together and in one piece! Well done. It's at around this stage of the whole divorce experience that many people ask the same question…

"What now?"

Here's a letter I received recently that highlights the sort of thing I'm talking about. It's from Mark Baker, a thirty-four-year-old man from Glasgow in Scotland. He attended one of my talks and decided to write to me. **His divorce went well**, he sees a lot of his children and is on good terms with his wife. Work is fine, he was recently promoted to area manager for both Glasgow and Edinburgh and he's looking forward to a **canoeing** holiday with friends in Mid Wales, yet still he's unhappy as he wonders what to do next. Over to you, Mark…

Dear Keith,

Hello, my name is Mark Baker. I'm thirty-four years old. I came to see you giving one of your talks earlier this year and thought that you might be able to help.

I am recently divorced and I suppose I have to say that it went very well. I see a lot of my children and get on well with my ex wife. At work things are very good; I was recently promoted to area manager for both Glasgow and Edinburgh. Later this year I'm going to Mid Wales for a canoeing holiday with friends yet I'm still unhappy as I wonder what to do next; where to take my life. I was hoping that you might be able to help.

Regards,

Mark Baker

Hmm, what do you think? How do you react, after reading this much of the book, to Mark's dilemma? I think your reactions can be **broken down** as follows:

- Why is he not happy?

- How could he be happier?

- Isn't his handwriting similar to the other letter writers?

All perfectly understandable reactions, but I was more concerned with something else. What got my alarm bells ringing was the **sudden mention of suicide** in the last but one line. I couldn't understand why someone with so much to live for would suddenly talk about a desire to "take my life". Then again, of course, Mark does hail from Glasgow in Scotland and as we established earlier in the book (Step 1, Something's Not Right), it is the dour Scots who are most likely to *do something silly*. Mark's words seem to bear out the research, which is a great shame, as on many levels he seems to have so much to live for. Still, the letter is **a cry for help** and as such shall not go unanswered.

If he *is* set on ending it all then it is my pleasure to offer up a list of options to answer the question, "Where can I take my life?" **Nowadays there are many and varied ways of ending it all; I've listed some of the more obvious traditional ones and also a few newer, more left field ways:**

Goodbye Cruel World!

- Pills

- Firearms

- Tall buildings

- In front of a bus (moving)

- In the bath

- Beachy Head

- Strangulation

- Drowning

- Mass events, organized on the internet

- Joining a religious cult. As the FBI are banging on the door
  you drink down the hastily distributed sleeping draught,
  with the promise of reuniting with your glorious leader in
  the 6th dimension.

All the above are ways to consider if you've *reached the end
of your tether*. If you have, then one of the last things to feel is
alone: you are in fine company. Through the ages, many of
the great and good have chosen the last resort as a last resort
or their way of bidding adieu to this life; here is a smattering:

- Adolph Hitler

- Rudolph Hess

- Joseph Goebbels

- Heinrich Himmler

- Herve Villechaize (*Fantasy Island*)

"Keith, Keith! What are you saying? Are you encouraging poor Mark to commit suicide?" Of course I'm not, only a fool would play with fire in that way; what I'm actually doing is **something much cleverer**, I'm carrying out an intervention! Shocking him into his senses by going along with his wishes. I'm sure that if he's mentioned his plans to friends, they'll have said something like, "No, Mark, don't do it! Please, don't!" If anything this will only have encouraged him. On the other hand, my approach will wrong-foot him and make him stop dead in his tracks and take stock.

Like trying to get a small child to eat broccoli, sometimes it's psychological warfare. With my little smashers I well remember trying to persuade them of the health benefits of vegetables in general, to no avail; it was a constant battle, and one that I was losing, until one day I turned the whole situation on its head. I denied them vegetables, telling them that they weren't old enough yet. Only "big boys" could eat vegetables in this house! You should have seen them; **they went ballistic!** The table was upturned, food went everywhere, and voices were raised. But they ate the vegetables! All of them! It was a hit, a success, a triumph! In one afternoon I had turned around their eating habits through the simple technique of reverse psychology. I'll never forget Marion's face when she got home later that day and untied me; absolute delight… As the *EasteEnders* might say, "Sorted!"

So, Mark, go on, do it! You know what? I don't think you're big enough! *Not* not big enough to commit suicide, of course you're big enough for that, **there's no height restriction**; see Herve Villechaize (above). No, I mean not big enough to *carry on living*, like the rest of the grown-ups! You just haven't got it in you, you big wet blanket! Death is the best thing for you! **Don't worry, I'm just goading him into taking an anti-suicide stance, like Mel Gibson at the beginning of one of the *Lethal Weapon* films where he forces the depressed man to jump off the building with him.** Mark will be infuriated by my words, he will now see living as a challenge to be conquered. But what if this doesn't work? OK, let's try another method; who remembers *Word Switching* from earlier in the book? We've already referred to suicide as doing something silly, in an effort to take the sting out of its tail. Well, let's Word Switch again, but this time let's switch to a different word. How about this?

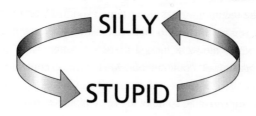

Do you see? By the clever use of Word Switching, we've taken the light-hearted element out of suicide and reinforced the fact that it is actually **a terrible thing** to do, a *bad* thing to do… a **STUPID** thing to do! Now take that word, stupid, and turn it into a mantra. Picture the word in your head, imagine that it's made out of huge pieces of rock or, if you're a music fan, imagine it in big red neon lettering like Elvis (Presley) had in his 1968 Comeback Special. Picture it in your mind; see it, huge red letters flashing on and off. Remember that it's STUPID that we want to see, not ELVIS. As you see the word in your mind, begin to say it to yourself, "Stupid, stupid, stupid, stupid, stupid, stupid, stupid, stupid, stupid… etc." How do you feel now? Exactly, stupid! Who wants to do something they know is stupid? No one!

Problem over.

Full Steam Ahead

And so we enter a new chapter (of your life, not the book. In terms of the book this is just a new part of the same chapter…) that will contain challenges aplenty. I know that if you use the techniques that I have taught you in *Making Divorce Work*, you will be able to make not just your divorce, but also your whole life work. Indeed, there is a danger with a book like this that you could become *too* happy, *too* contented, *too* well adjusted if you're not careful! If you feel that is a possibility, simply re-read some of the key chapters and do exactly the opposite of what I suggest.

It's a bit of fun!

So, to return to my earlier question, "What now?" Well, that's up to you and, depending on the size of the financial responsibility of your divorce settlement, and your ex-wife (or husband, but probably wife). How much you have to pay out every month in spousal maintenance will have an effect on what you can or cannot do with your life now. But **is money that important?** Is it the be all and end all that dictates the extent to which you can enjoy your life and experience for the first time a sense of dignity, bringing to an end the overwhelming feeling of self-loathing? I think so, yes. **There's no such thing as a free lunch**; supermarkets often give out little nibbles for free but they are at best a snack, far from a balanced meal. Having said that, I know for a fact that in parts of London like the Embankment free meals are regularly given out to the homeless. Ironically many of the poor, **filthy hobos** are only living rough after disastrous, painful marriages that end with them splitting from their wives. In all honesty who can blame their wives for leaving them, frankly many of them are very shabby and stink of booze. In that sense, we can see that divorcing can often mean a fast track to a free meal. Speaking of freedom, your freedom will have cost you, both emotionally and financially, but I urge you not to let that hold you back. Now that you are **sailing out of the port of divorce** you can steam on to the dry land of happiness at a rate of knots, being careful not to run aground on the sandbank of alimony, sunning yourself on the poop deck as you go! As you embark on this sea quest, please think of *Making Divorce Work* as your breadfruit and vitamin C. Now that you are actively searching for a new mate, the **last thing you need is scurvy**. But at which islands of opportunity and experience do you want to drop your anchor? After all the emotional upheaval you've been through, you hardly want to just drift around without a care in the world. It's important to know where you want to go; **it's important to set goals**.

Goals

"Such a perfect day"

DURAN DURAN – PERFECT DAY

"I'm not perfect, but I'm perfect for you"

GRACE JONES – I'M NOT PERFECT

"It's got to be… perfect"

FAIRGROUND ATTRACTION – PERFECT

In his wonderful book, *Change Your Life in Seven Days*, Paul McKenna talks about the importance of setting goals; he calls them *"the servants of a better life"*. What does he mean by that? Well, one thing's for sure; **he's not advocating slavery**. He's not jumping up on his soapbox and preaching a return to the dark days of Deep South plantation-based **systematic racism**; he would never say that. I think what he's actually saying is that goals can help us all to enjoy better lives and that, like servants, they can bring the better things to us. Paul would be the first person to admit that he himself has set goals in his life, not least to have a number one bestselling self-help book. Of course he has achieved that goal with *Change Your Life in Seven Days*, it's a runaway hit; I wouldn't be at all surprised though to hear that a **perfectionist** like Paul McKenna lies awake at night **kicking** himself for not whittling away at the book for that little bit longer and getting it down to **six days!** But there we are, that's **the danger of perfectionism**, the chance that nothing, no matter how hard you try, will ever be good enough for you. Look at Van Gogh (another suicide), I wonder if he had as high an opinion of his *Sunflowers* as we do? Probably not; there must have been loads of occasions when he looked at the canvas and just saw a pile of badly drawn daffodils. Did Sylvia Plath (another one) chuckle merrily at *The Bell Jar* or did she just see a mess of punctuation and letters? We'll never know. What we do know is that all three of them, Vincent Van Gogh, Sylvia Plath and Paul McKenna, **set themselves goals on an almost daily basis** and it worked for them. Only a fool would speculate that the suicides themselves were also goals, but I think it's worth considering. The tragic Sylvia Plath has the added honour of being portrayed on film by Gwyneth Paltrow. It's tantalizing to think that, had she lived, we may have been fortunate enough to hear her words put to music by Chris Martin for his band The Coldplay and played to a crowd of thousands at a massive Free Trade benefit concert with support spots from Travis and Shaggy. It wasn't to be.

What Goals?

We've seen how **important** it is to set goals in our lives, but **what exactly should those goals involve?** Should they be small goals, easily achievable? Middle size, fairly challenging goals or **crazy, pie in the sky madness** that you haven't got a hope in hell of achieving? What do you think? Which one, in your opinion, is the best choice? Have you made your choice? OK, I'm willing to bet that you chose either the small or middle size goal because you thought they were more achievable; after all, what chance would you have of achieving "crazy, pie in the sky madness"?

Do you know what my answer is to that? **Plenty**. **Plenty chance**.

"The bigger the goal the better!"

That's what I say. The bigger the goal, the easier it is to score. Footballers know this to be true; they would sell their grannies to have bigger goals. *Not all footballers, obviously. I'm talking primarily about midfield and attacking players. For defenders and goalkeepers the notion of bigger goals is an absolute nightmare. Appalling. Also it wouldn't work for any adopted players, they would have to sell a legal guardian; but you take my point…* "The bigger the better!" That's what they'd say if you asked them, and so should you. **Make your goals enormous**. Look at rock sensation Darius Danesh; he could have quite easily drifted through life with a goal no bigger than wanting to sing a Britney Spears song on television while sporting **ridiculous facial hair**. That would have been enough for some people, but not for Darius, he was aiming higher. He wanted to do something that would make a difference to the world. Unlike Paul McKenna, who takes a quieter, subtler stance in his fight against a return to slavery, Darius locked himself in his room and (ironically) slaved away for days with his pen and pad until he had produced a song that was to change the way we think about race. "Colour Blind" was released to a waiting world on 29 July 2002, and whilst I don't know that much about music, I know what I like; we'll be humming this one for years to come, regardless of our skin tone. Darius had achieved both his goals and so can you, but **not until you know what your goal is**. There are as many different goals as there are people. Take your family as an example; each member will harbour their own dreams. "Wait a minute, Keith. I thought we were talking about goals, not dreams. What the heck are you playing at?"

Ah! That's my point! Don't you see? Goals *are* dreams! There, is it becoming clearer? We all have dreams. What are yours?

- To score the winning goal at the FA Cup Final? *Actually that's a bad example, I'm overplaying the "goal" card.*

- Winning Wimbledon? The tennis show, not the South London borough.

- To raise a happy family?

- To steer the *QE2* into Sydney harbour?

- To reintroduce free milk into Britain's schools?

- If you're a lady, to win Miss World?

- To host a revival of the BBC's *The Great Egg Race*?

- To sing with The Red Hot Chilli Peppers?

- To find a cure for smallpox?

- To run a marathon?

- To do a bungee jump?

- To own a DVD player?

- To join an adult education course?

What a great set of goals! What a great set of dreams! And do you know what? There's no reason for you **not to achieve** them. Years ago we thought it was impossible to run a mile in four minutes; why, some people found it hard just running *for* four minutes. Then Roger Bannister did it and whoosh! A dream had come true. Nowadays lots of people have done it although to be honest it's still **beyond most people** and should only be attempted if you're at the peak of your fitness. There are certain groups that should give this a wide berth: asthmatics, diabetics, the morbidly obese and, nowadays, Roger Bannister. Mind you, in the case of the morbidly obese, they have to give everything a wide berth.

It's a bit of fun.

"Any dream will do"

STEPHEN GATELY – *JOSEPH AND HIS AMAZING TECHNICOLOR DREAM COAT*

So the time has come to choose your goal, the time has come to choose your dream! Are you excited? You should be…

OK, put on your glasses.

I want you to imagine that you are in a fine restaurant, sat at a table laid out with the best silverware and goblets full of very old wine. As you look around you notice that the restaurant is full of famous people: there's Lord Nelson, there's JFK, look, it's Judy Finnegan! You sit in your plush, red velvet seat and the waiter approaches with a menu, but it's not a menu of food, it's **a menu of dreams!** *A Dream Menu!* As you read it you realize that it contains every dream imaginable, and then some! *What can I get you, sir?* enquires the crusty old retainer; how do you reply?

- *Bring me it all!*

- *I want everything!*

- *Sorry, could I have a few more minutes?*

Amazing! What a restaurant! It's a smorgasbord! Now when you think of your future, post divorce, imagine that you are sitting at the best table in the restaurant, choosing your dream. Once you have made your choice, tell "the waiter" (your mind) which meal you've chosen (which dream) and get ready to eat it (act it out) **FOR THE REST OF YOUR LIFE!**

Whilst I encourage you to write down your dreams and to act on them, I have to point out at this stage that if a goal is a dream, then just like a bad dream (being chased through a forest on a bike, drowning in an enormous bucket of milk, getting trapped inside a red post box and concussed by a falling postcard, walking through the high street without your trousers on, hurting a bear … that sort of thing), it's also possible to have **bad goals**. Having **bad goals** is the equivalent of a superhero using his powers for evil, and though I don't approve of censorship, I do in this case and have to take a stand against **bad goals**. "Fine Keith, that's hardly a surprise; we're *all* against **bad goals**, but sometimes it can be hard to tell the bad from the good. What, in your opinion, Keith, constitutes a **bad goal**?"

Well, we all have our own ideas of what a bad goal is. There are as many bad goals as there are bad people. Here are a few that I think are awful.

1. To become the biggest drug dealer in the North East of England, with a massive network of underworld contacts

that spreads overseas. Hiding the cash in offshore banks or postal accounts with a slightly higher rate of interest than an over-the-counter variety.

2. To hold the record for the largest number of hostages taken at any one time.

3. To become the first person to swear on the mid-week Lottery draw, televised live to the nation.

These are, by anyone's standard, very bad goals, **bordering on evil**. Now let's do an exercise together. Get a pen or pencil (not a felt tip or marker pen, it will show through on the other side) and write down three of your own *bad goals* on the next page. Three of the very worst things you could aspire to in life. Then follow it up with three *good goals*. Take your time to come up with three things that are personal to you, don't just copy mine. Unless they happen to match yours in which case feel free.

MY THREE BAD GOALS

1

2

3

MY THREE GOOD GOALS

1

2

3

Now that you have these two very special lists, you are in your strongest position yet to look at your life as it is *right now*, at this very moment, and make a definite judgement as to where you're at and just how bad things really are.

Look at both of the lists at the same time. What do they tell you about **your personality?** Do they surprise you? They shouldn't, they're *your* lists and therefore *your* goals. Now that you've grown in confidence, use the two lists as a map to consult as you **ramble onward** into this new, happier period of your life, ready to start a new relationship fully armed with the knowledge you have acquired from *Making Divorce Work*. Think of the good goals as **your directions**, and the bad goals as warning signs of areas to avoid, like an oil spill, an old uncovered mineshaft or an unsafe bridge. Above all, USE the lists. As with all the excellent advice that I have dispensed throughout the book, reading it is only the first part of the process. In fact it's not even the first part, it's a *part* of the first part; you'll have to read everything several times for it to sink in, then you'll have to *act on it*.

Action!

This is vital. Think of it as once again being in a wonderful restaurant. All around you are fantastic dishes, cooked to perfection; as you breathe in through your nose, your senses come alive! You take some time to peruse the menu, choosing carefully from its mouth-watering array. You make your choice, the dish arrives, but until you've eaten it you won't have had the full experience, or seen the full picture. **You have to follow through**. Who was it that once said, **"A winner never quits, and a quitter never wins"**? Most recently me, and I think I'm right.

In many ways it's **like being an actor** who has been given the greatest script ever written. He can read the script and know it's good; he can learn the script and know it's good; but until he **acts the script** he's not going to feel like the part or play it convincingly. Even when he knows the part off by heart, he may *still* not play it convincingly; I'm thinking of *Hollyoaks*. It's like the phrase that youngsters and gangster wrappers use, *"You can talk the talk, but can you walk the walk?"* or *"Tell it to the face, because my hand isn't listening!"* In other words, **you have to start to implement my advice**. Now!

Role-play

You are in a restaurant; you are alone and hungry. The restaurant is one of the finest in the country and the smell of beautifully prepared food is heavy in the air.

The waiter approaches.

WAITER Good evening, sir. Would you like to see the menu?

YOU Yes please, that would be very nice, thank you.

The waiter hands you the menu; you take it and smile.

YOU Thank you, that's lovely. Thank you.

As you read the menu you hear the waiter begin to talk...

WAITER Our special today is the sea bass. Why don't you have that?

YOU Mmm, sea bass... Yes, I like sea bass. Thank you, I'll have the sea bass, that'll be lovely. Sea bass. I'm looking forward to my sea bass.

The waiter notes your order and leaves. He returns five minutes later with a beautiful, freshly cooked sea bass; he places it on the table in front of you. Which of the following three replies do you give?

A:
Mmm, sea bass, lovely, thank you very much. Here I go, tucking into my sea bass.

B:
That's fine, just leave it there but I doubt that I'll eat it. The important part was ordering it.

C:
This is not what I ordered. I'm allergic to sea bass.

Which reply did you choose? Each reply will say something different about you. I wish there was some way of knowing what you chose. If you ever bump into me on your travels please remember which choice you made and we can have a chat about it then. Good luck!

NOW I KNOW

✱ Goals are good; make yours big.
Aim for something you know you'll never achieve!

✱ Suicide is rarely the answer.

✱ Ordering the food is only the first step of the journey.

✱ Vegetables can be fun.

9

The Quiz

*This book has by now armed
you with everything you need
to know about the exciting
world of separation.*

*To see exactly how much you have
learned you should answer all the
following Yes / No questions.*

*Be honest with your answers, if not
it will only be yourself you are cheating.*

1. ARE YOU MALE?

a. Yes Keith. Yes Keith I am male, I am a man. (I could be a boy but it is far more likely I am a man). Happy to be a man. I am at ease with my male gender. Yes.

b. No

2. ARE YOU MARRIED?

a. Yes Keith I am. I have met a wonderful person. I have committed myself for life to my significant other. I am happy to confirm my married status. I can safely say I'm feeling a little smug with myself.

b. No

3. ARE YOU DIVORCED?

a. Well you are a little blunt in your asking, I have no problem answering your questions but is it right to just blurt them out? I am fine but others might be more fragile. It's not the nicest thing in the world to have thrown at you. But if you are insisting I answer then it's easiest just to say yes. Not my fault. But yes. OK it was six of one half a dozen of the other. It does take two to tango.

b. No

4 ARE YOU ROMANTIC?

a. Given the opportunity. Yes. But you must realize in this day and age sending gifts and letters to people unsolicited can often be misinterpreted. I think if the first two bouquets and heart-shaped balloons haven't worked it's very unlikely you will get any positive response, you're barking up the wrong tree and the whole thing is probably going to end in tears. Out of your league pal out of your league. However I think everyone enjoys a sunset.

b. No

5. DO YOU HAVE A HIGH SEX DRIVE?

a. That's it, isn't it? It's all some people think about. You soften me up with questions about romance then go straight for the juggler. In this area I am completely normal. Happily normal. What's normal? Well, I suppose above average covers it. I will not be made to look a fool by the likes of you.

b. No

6. ARE YOU A PARENT?

a. This is a lovely question. Happy to answer this one. In fact you can get rid of most of the rubbish you're asking and ask me this dozens of time. Yes I am a parent. A happy parent with smashing children that are a credit to me. Sometimes they can get a little out of hand, but that's high spirits, a lot of the playing fields have been sold off by the schools so is it any wonder they have so much excess energy? I really think my kids are beginning to turn a corner and we can put it all behind us. Moving to a completely new area seemed at first to be an admission of failure but I think it's given the whole family a much needed shot in the arm. (Which is ironic in itself if you think about where it all started.)

b. No

7. DO YOU BELIEVE MEN AND WOMEN ARE EQUAL?

a. Yes of course. If you got on the wrong side of my mother she should give you a hell of a wallop, whereas my dad seemed to be in his own little world. He loved his gardening.

b. No

8. DO YOU HAVE A PET?

a. Not officially, the landlord doesn't want animals in the house, but I have smuggled in a gerbil. It's for the kids really. When they come to visit it helps make the place feel more like home.

b. No

9. ARE YOU HAPPY?
a. Mustn't grumble. I'll be honest the last couple of years have been a real kick in the pants. But what is happy? I've got a few quid left at the end of the week and a 36" plasma screen in the front room. So things can't be that bad.

b. No

10. ARE YOU IN LOVE?

a. Trick question, impossible to say at this stage. It's early days and I don't want to jinx it.

b. No

11. ARE YOU SEPARATED?

a. Yes, well when you say 'separated' it sort of suggests that it's over but that the blow is being softened by an artificial period of delay that gives me the chance to get used to my loved one shacking up with someone else. I resent you implying that it's all over. If you knew how strongly we feel for each other you wouldn't even ask that. It's just so difficult sometimes, I just feel overwhelmed.

b. No

12. DO YOU AVOID CONFLICT IN A RELATIONSHIP?

a. I never start it if that's what you mean. But if trouble rears its head then I won't back down. Why should I? I live here too. I pay half the bills. If someone (who shall remain nameless) could handle their drink then there would be no rows at all. But of course it's all my fault, I make them feel confined and a drink in the evening is the only thing that makes them feel young again. Well I'm the one who has to clean it up.

b. No

13. ARE YOU HEALTHY?

a. Yes. I certainly try to exercise and watch my weight. I tried the Atkins but I never really got on with it. Actually it never got on with me. I have stopped taking sugar in my tea and I am thinking of doing a fun run.

b. No

14. ARE YOU COMPETITIVE?

a. I don't think it's a problem. I like to win but I'm not mad about it. What is the point of entering a competition if you don't try and win? I think it's important to teach children to lose gracefully. If that makes me some kind of lunatic so be it.

b. No

15. DO YOU *SEEK* CONFLICT IN A RELATIONSHIP?

a. Here we go. What's been said? Is this about Christmas? All I said was that I'm not staying for a week with a family that obviously doesn't approve of me. If they want to see their grandchildren that much they can travel down and stay in the spare bedroom. I don't care what they say, she is only 67 and I've seen her sprinting downstairs when *EastEnders* comes on so I think it's a bit far fetched to pretend she can't use public transport. I suppose this counts as a YES by your standards. Typical.

b. No

HOW DID YOU SCORE?

Mainly Yes

Very well done, you're honest. Maybe a little too honest. Perhaps it would be worth having a long hard look at yourself and see why you're pushing the world away. On the other hand you might not want to.

Mainly No

Why don't you come down from that ivory tower once in a while and smell the coffee? If you spent less time looking down your nose at everyone else you might see that you're not so perfect yourself. On the other hand you may be perfectly happy. And that's ok.

Half and Half

Lovely. What a nice, even-tempered, easy-going individual you are. No problem. Unless of course you have a problem, in which case get help as soon as you can.

BIBLIOGRAPHY

I have started the bibliography with a section of off colour humour, what I call "humour in poor taste". I hope that this serves as compensation for those readers who were expecting more of that sort of thing in *Making Divorce Work*. Most of these titles are available on Amazon, some of them though are out of print and can only be found in musty old second hand bookshops. If you are interested in second hand bookshops I recommend a visit to the beautiful town of Hay on Wye in my native Wales. This little town, tucked away in the Welsh hills is an oasis for book lovers and ramblers alike. If you've never been to Wales, this is as good a place as any to start. *Bon Voyage!*

That's French, but you take my point.

Some places to stay: The Swan at Hay Hotel (01497 821188), Kilverts Hotel (01497 821042), The Famous Old Black Lion (01497 820841) (I'd never heard of it), Seven Stars Hotel *indoor pool, sauna, car park* (01497 820886)

Or visit the web site, www.hay-on-wye.co.uk

Off Colour Humour

- *The Big Book Of Filth* by Jonathon Green, Kipper Williams (Cassell Reference)
- *Dirty Cockney Rhyming Slang* (Michael O'Mara Books)
- *The F-word* by Jesse Sheidlower (Faber and Faber)
- *That's Disgusting: An Adult Guide To What's Gross, Tasteless, Crude, Rude and Lewd* by Greta Garbage (Ten Speed Press)
- *Can I Have My Balls Back Please?* by Dotun Adebayo (The X Press)
- *Dirty Words Of Wisdom: A Treasury Of Classic ?*$@! Quotations* by Sam Stall, Lou Harry (Chronicle Books)
- *The Best Adult Joke Book Ever* by Johnny Sharpe, Emma Hayley (Arcturus Publishing)
- *The Solo Sex Joke Book: Jokes, Cartoons and Limericks About The World's Most Popular Sex Act* by Ralph Mead (Editor) and Christian Snyder (Illustrator) (Factor Press)
- *The Dirty Joke Book* by Mr "K" (Citadel Press)
- *The Little Book Of Gay Gags* by Michael Green and John Jensen (Robson Books)

Despair and Abandonment

- *When Your Lover Leaves You: Six Stages to Recovery and Growth* by Richard G. Whiteside and Frances E. Steinberg (Golden Books Adult Publishing)
- *When Things Fall Apart* by Pema Chodron (Thorsons)
- *How to Mend Your Broken Heart* by Paul McKenna and Hugh Wilbourn (Bantam Press)

- *Codependendent's Guide to the Twelve Steps: How to Find the Right Programme for You* by Melody Beattie (Simon & Schuster)
- *Beyond Codependency: And Getting Better All the Time!* by Melody Beattie (Hazelden Information & Educational Services)
- *Letting Go of Anxiety and Depression* by Windy Dryden (Sheldon Press)
- *The Little Book of Letting Go: A Revolutionary 30-day Program to Cleanse Your Mind, Lift Your Spirit and Replenish Your Soul* by High Prather (Vermillion)
- *Happiness Is the Best Revenge: 50 Ways to Let Go of the Past and Find Happiness Now* by Chuck Spezzano (Hodder Mobius)
- *By the River I Sat Down and Wept* by Paulo Coelho (HarperCollins)
- *Despair* by Vladmimir Nabokov (Penguin Modern Classics)
- *Abandon Every Hope* by Wilhelm Waitz (PublishAmerica)

Healing
- *Aromatherapy* by Julia Lawless (Thorsons)
- *Crystal Healing* by Simon Lilly (Thorsons)
- *Nude Work Out 8 – Naked Yoga, including introduction to power yoga* (NB Video, and not suitable for persons under 18) (HE Productions)
- *Aromatherapy for Healing the Spirit: Restoring Emotional and Mental Balance with Essential Oils* by Gabriel Moja (Inner Traditions International)
- *Reflexology* by Inge Dougans (Thorsons)

- *Why Am I So Tired: Is Your Thyroid Making You Ill?* By Martin Budd N.D., D.O. (Thorsons)
- *The IBS Breakthrough: Healing Irritable Bowel Syndrome for Good with Ancient Chinese Medicine* by Leigh Fortson and Bing Lee (Fair Winds Press)
- *First Aid Manual* by St Andrews' Ambulance Association and the British Red Cross St John Ambulance (Dorling Kindersley)

Personal Growth

- *Embraced by the Light* by Betty J Eadie (HarperCollins)
- *Change Your Life in Seven Days* by Paul McKenna (Bantam Press)
- *The Paranormal World of Paul McKenna* by Paul McKenna (Faber and Faber)
- *The Hypnotic World of Paul McKenna* by Paul McKenna (Faber and Faber)
- *Head First* by Tony Buzan (Thorsons)
- *Head Strong* by Tony Buzan (Thorsons)
- *Head Injury: A Practical Guide* by Trevor Powell (Speechmark Publishing)
- *Help Yourself* by Dave Pelzer (Thorsons)
- *Jonathan Livingston Seagull* by Richard Bach (HarperCollins)
- *Boost Your Self Esteem* by Pete Cohen (HarperCollins)
- *How to Become More Interesting* by Edward de Bono (Penguin)
- *If Only* by Geri Halliwell (Bantam)
- *5 Easy Steps to Becoming a Witch* by Gilly Sergiev (HarperCollins)

Deal With Change And Stress

- *Who Moved my Cheese?* by Spencer Johnson (Calendar)

- *Free Yourself from Harmful Stress* by Trevor Powell (Dorling Kindersley)

- *Healing Without Freud or Prozac: Natural Approaches to Conquering Stress, Anxiety, Depression Without Drugs and Without Psychotherapy* by David Servan-Schreiber (Rodale)

- *Plato not Prozac* by Lou Marinoff (HarperCollins)

- *Potatoes not Prozac* by Kathleen Desmaisons (Pocket Books)

- *Making the Prozac Decision: Guide to Anti-Depressants* by Carol Turkington (Contemporary Books)

Second Thoughts?

- *How to Win Your Lover Back and Keep the One You Love: It's Not Over!* by David Randall Brown (Randall)

- *How One of You Can Bring the Two of You Together* by Susan Page (Broadway Books)

- *How to Get Your Lover Back* by Blase Harris (Dell Publishing)

- *Obsessive Love: When It Hurts Too Much to Let it Go* by Susan Forward (Bantam)

- *Surviving a Stalker: Everything You Need to Know to Keep Yourself Safe* by Linden Gross (Marlowe & Company)

Fun, Friendship And More...

- *First Impressions: What You Don't Know About How Others See You* by Ann Demarais and Valerie White (Hodder Mobius)

- *How to Talk to Women* by Ron Louis and Dave Copeland (Mastery Technologies Press)

- *Are You the One for Me?* by Barbara De Angelis (HarperCollins)

- *How to Make Anyone Like You: Proven Ways to Become a People Magnet* by Leil Lowndes (HarperCollins)

- *How to Make People Like You in 90 Seconds or Less* by Nicholas Boothman (Workmen Publishing)

- *Talk to ME: Conversation Tips for the Small-Talk Challenged* by Carole Honeychurch and Angela Watrous (New Harbinger Publications)

- *How to Make Anyone Fall in Love With You: 85 Proven Techniques for Success* by Leil Lowndes (HarperCollins)

- *Updating!: How to Win a Man or Woman You Thought You Could Never Get* by Leil Lowndes (Contemporary Books)

- *The Bluffer's Guide to Ballet: Bluff Your Way in Ballet* by Craig Dodd (Oval Books)

- *How to Break Your Addiction to a Person* by Howard M Halpern (Bantam)

- *He's Scared, She's Scared: Understanding the Hidden Fears that Sabotage Your Relationships*, by Stephen Carter and Julia Sokel (Bantam Press)

Little Smashers

- *Confident Children* by Gael Lindenfield (HarperCollins)
- *Men Are from Mars, Women Are from Venus, Children Are from Heaven* by John Gray (Thorsons)
- *The Sixty Minute Father* by Rob Parsons (Hodder & Stoughton)
- *Freeing Ourselves From The Mad Myths Of Parenthood!* by Susan Jeffers (Hodder Mobius)
- *Divorced Dad's Survival Book* by David Knox and Kermitt Leggett (Perseus)
- *It's Not Your Fault, Koko Bear: A Read-Together Book for Parents and Young Children During Divorce* by Vicky Lansky (Book Peddlers)
- *Where's Daddy? Separation and Your Child* by Jill Curtis and Virginia Elllis (Bloomsbury)
- *Do U Know Who Your Daddy Is?* by Robert Montogomery (1st Books Library)

Diet

- *Easy Gluten-Free Cooking* by Rita Greer (HarperCollins)
- *The Good Gut Guide* by Stephanie Zinser, Foreword by Prof R John Nicholls (HarperCollins)
- *Irritable Bowel Syndrome and Diverticulosis* by Shirley Trickett (HarperCollins)

- *Healthy Cooking for Two (or Just You!)* by Frances Price (Rodale Press)
- *Quick and Easy Microwave Cooking for One* by Rena Croft and Catherine Atkinson *(Quick & Easy Series)*

Get Out and About!

- *Pembrokeshire Coast* by Alf Anderson, John Cleare and Ian Mercer (David and Charles)
- *Dining Out in Wales: A Guide to the Best in Wales* (Welsh Development Agency)
- *The M4 Motorway (Severn Bridge) (Speed Limit) Regulations 1995: Road Traffic (Statutory Instruments: 1995: 2168)* (The Stationery Office Books)
- *Collins Road Atlas: Britain* (HarperCollins)
- *1001 Days Out with Your Kids* (Parragon Publishing)
- *Travelling Solo: Advice and Ideas for More Than 250 Great Holidays* by Eleanor Berman (Globe Pequot Press)

In the Club

- *Best is Yet to Come: Coping with Divorce and Enjoying Life Again* by Ivana Trump (Pocket Books)
- *Fools Rush In* by Anthea Turner (Little, Brown)
- *Cher: If You Believe* by Mark Bego (Cooper Square Press)
- *Richard and Judy: The Autobiography* by Judy Finnigan and Richard Madeley (Coronet)

- *Lulu: I Don't Want to Fight* by "Lulu" (Time Warner Paperbacks)
- *Diana: Her True Story - In Her Own Words* by Andrew Morton (Michael O'Mara Books)
- *Six Wives: The Queens of Henry VIII* by David Starkey (Vintage)

Desert Island Divorce

- *The Complete Works of William Shakespeare* by William Shakespeare, edited by Peter Alexander (HarperCollins)
- *The Bible*

AND

- *Great Expectations* by Charles Dickens (Penguin Popular Classics)

OR

- *War and Peace* by Leo Tolstoy (Wordsworth Classics)

OR

- *The Day of the Triffids* by John Wyndham (Penguin)